HOLD WITHOUT PANIC

How To Swing Trade 2-3 Hours Per Week While Working Full-Time

Jeff Qualls

ISBN: 979-8-218-93899-4

Published by: Operator Publishing

Disclaimer:

Trading involves substantial risk. This book is intended solely for educational purposes. Past performance does not guarantee future results. The author is not a licensed financial advisor. All trading decisions are the sole responsibility of the reader.

First Edition: April 2026

Contents

INTRODUCTION

Day trading promises freedom but often delivers stress, screen addiction, and burnout. Swing trading delivers consistency, calm, and time — without quitting your job, your family, or your sleep.

This book is for people who:

- Have tried (or considered) day trading and found it unsustainable with a job and family life.

- Want to participate in the markets but refuse to sacrifice evenings, weekends, or sleep.

- Are ready to shift from excitement-driven trading to a rules-based, low-time-commitment system.

You will learn the OPERATOR Swing Trading System — a structured approach focused on position management, risk control, and calm execution. It is built for people with full-time jobs, limited time, and a preference for results over excitement.

This is not a get-rich-quick book. It is a practical guide for part-time traders who treat trading like a side business: disciplined, intentional, and sustainable.

What You Get

- Clear rules (8 core rules) eliminate most emotional decisions.

- A weekly routine requiring only 2–3 hours total.

- Tools to qualify setups, size positions safely, set exits in advance, and review performance without obsession.

- Real examples from part-time traders who succeeded while keeping full-time jobs.

> **INCLUDES FREE COMPANION WORKBOOK**
> Download your 35-page Execution Workbook at: Operator Trading.com/workbook that includes: Setup Gate checklists, position-sizing calculator, trade-execution logs, and weekly and monthly review templates. The book teaches the system. The workbook helps you execute it.

Let's begin by understanding why day trading fails so many capable people — and why swing trading fits real life better.

This book teaches you the OPERATOR swing trading system.

The workbook helps you EXECUTE it.

INCLUDED IN YOUR FREE DOWNLOAD:

✓ Complete Setup Gate Checklist — all 5 criteria with step-by-step verification

✓ Position Sizing Calculator — fill-in-the-blank formula for exact share count

✓ Trade Execution Logs — pre-formatted templates for every trade

✓ Weekly Review Templates — Friday checklist + monthly performance tracker

✓ Risk Management Worksheets — account, position, and trade-level calculators

Download Your Free Workbook:

OperatorTrading.com/workbook

Enter your email to receive instant access.

The book gives you the knowledge. The workbook gives you the structure.

Chapter 1

THE DAY TRADING TRAP

If you have attempted day trading and found yourself struggling, rest assured that you are not alone. Many aspiring traders enter the market with intelligence, discipline, and genuine commitment — and still lose money consistently. The problem is rarely the trader. It is the structure of day trading itself.

What Day Trading Actually Requires (That Most People Don't Have)

Day trading demands:

- 40+ hours per week glued to screens — often during regular work hours.

- High emotional tolerance for constant volatility and rapid decisions.

- At least $25,000 in account equity to avoid the Pattern Day Trader (PDT) rule, which restricts trading if you fall below this threshold.

- The ability to handle intense pressure without letting fear or greed override logic.

Most people already have full-time jobs, families, and normal stress limits. The mismatch is not a personal failing — it is structural. Day trading was not designed for working adults.

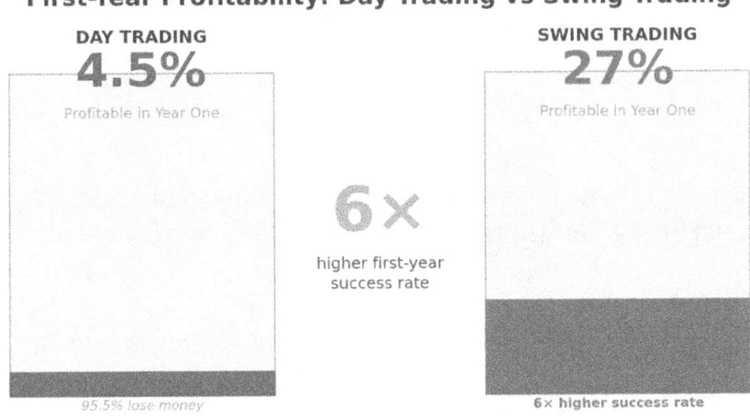

Caption: Day Trading: 4.5% profitable vs. Swing Trading: 27% profitable. Swing trading delivers a 6× higher first-year success rate. Source: Brokerage data analysis 2020–2025.

Caption: Day Trading: 40+ hours per week vs. Swing Trading: 2–3 hours per week. Swing trading requires 15× less time while maintaining consistent results.

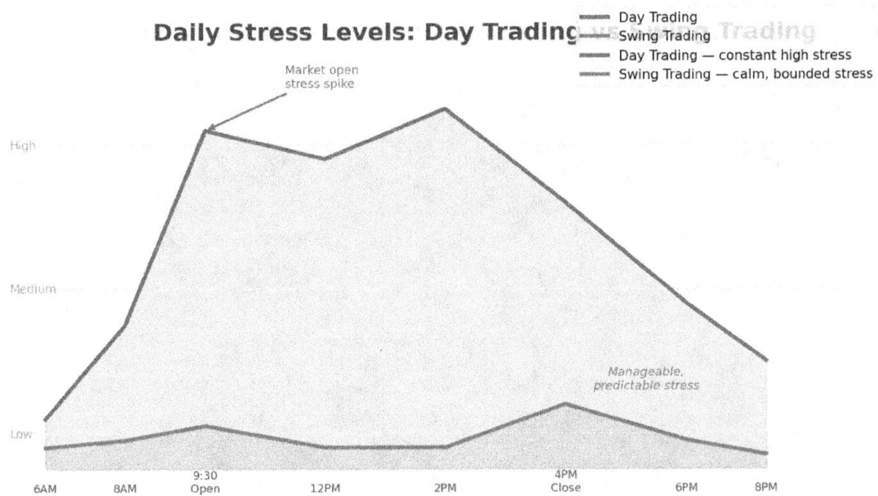

Caption: Day Trading maintains constant high-pressure stress throughout market hours. Swing Trading produces moderate, manageable stress with clear daily boundaries.

Caption: Day Trading minimum: $25,000+ with PDT restrictions. Swing Trading minimum: $5,000, no PDT rule — a 5× lower barrier to entry.

The Pivot to Swing Trading

Swing trading captures many of the same market moves but on a 2-to-20-day horizon. You scan for setups on Sunday evening, place orders on Monday, let them run during the week, and review results on Friday. Everything that makes day trading difficult is reduced or eliminated:

- You keep your job and evenings free.

- You sleep without worrying about overnight gaps — or at least with far less worry.

- You trade with calm discipline instead of constant adrenaline.

The system is built for consistency, not excitement. More activity is not more control. Day trading feels productive because you are constantly deciding. Swing trading is productive because you make a good decision once and then trust the process.

> **OPERATOR NOTE**
>
> More activity is not more control. Day trading feels productive because you are constantly deciding. Swing trading is productive because your decisions are made calmly on Sunday, not in the heat of Mondays open.

Reader Resources: Optional companion PDFs with scanner setup instructions and paper-trading templates are available at OperatorTrading.com/workbook.

Chapter 2

WHAT SWING TRADING ACTUALLY IS

Swing trading is not about trading less for the sake of trading less. It is about trading better — capturing meaningful market moves with fewer, higher-quality decisions. Where day trading reacts to every tick, swing trading anticipates multi-day trends and lets them develop without constant intervention.

The Weekly Routine — Simple and Repeatable

Swing trading means:

- Sunday evening: Scan for high-quality setups (30–60 minutes). Identify 3–5 potential trades that meet all 5 Setup Gate criteria.

- Monday morning: Check for triggers (10 minutes). Enter 1–2 positions if setups activate. Immediately set stop loss and profit target as GTC (good-til-canceled) orders.

- Tuesday–Friday: Check positions once per day after market close (5 minutes each day). Only act if the stop or target is hit.

- Friday: Perform weekly review (30 minutes). Log results, note patterns, and adjust watchlist for next week.

Total weekly time commitment: 2–3 hours.

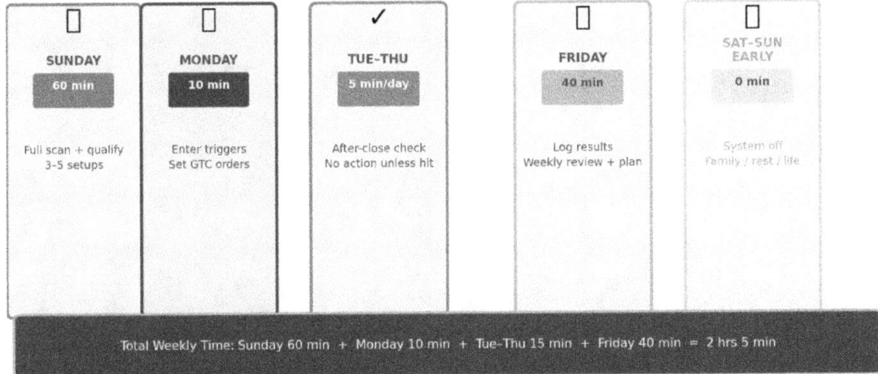

Caption: Complete weekly schedule: Sunday 60 min scan, Monday–Thursday 10 min/day, Friday 40 min including review. Total: 2.5 hours per week.

KEY INSIGHT

Swing trading is not about trading less. It is about trading better. You let positions develop without constant intervention, which means fewer emotional decisions and more consistent execution.

COMMON MISTAKE
"Swing trades typically develop over several days, meaning decisions are made during specific analysis windows rather than constant monitoring."

The Advantages in One View

Compared to day trading, swing trading removes:

- The $25,000 PDT minimum equity requirement.

- The need for constant screen time during market hours.

- The emotional rollercoaster of intraday volatility.

- The conflict with a full-time job or family responsibilities.

You still participate in the same markets. You still aim for positive expectancy. But you do it on terms that fit real life.

Chapter 3

THE TIME ADVANTAGE

Most traders fail not because they lack skill, but because they lack time. Day trading demands full-time attention during market hours — hours when most people are at work. Swing trading solves this problem by design.

The Actual Weekly Schedule

- Sunday evening: Scan charts and qualify setups (30–60 minutes). Mark 3–5 high-probability trades.

- Monday: Morning check for triggers (10 minutes). Enter positions, set stop and target orders (GTC), then close the platform.

- Tuesday–Thursday: One quick after-close check each day (5 minutes total per day). Confirm no stop or target hit; no action required otherwise.

- Friday: Weekly review (30 minutes). Log trades, analyze rule compliance, update watchlist.

Total: 2–3 hours per week. That is less time than most people spend scrolling social media or watching one TV episode per day.

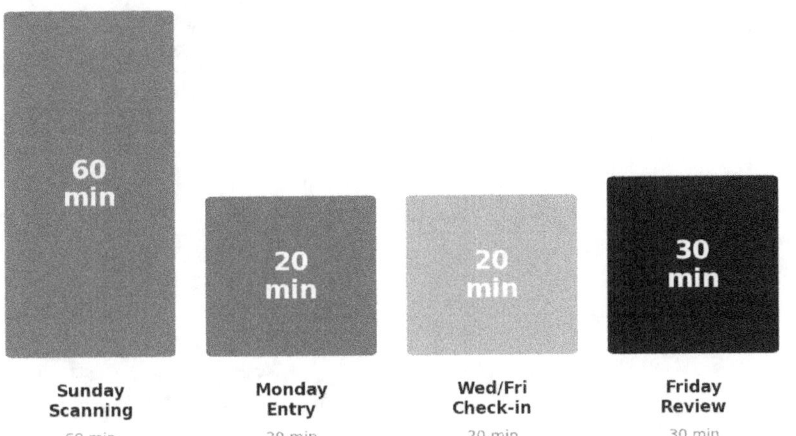

WEEKLY TIME COMMITMENT BREAKDOWN
Where your 2–3 hours actually go each week
60 min
20 min
20 min
30 min
Sunday Scanning
Monday Entry
Wed/Fri Check-in
Friday Review
60 min
20 min
20 min
30 min
Total: 130 minutes per week — less than a weekly Netflix episode
Time Commitment

THE OPERATOR WEEKLY SCHEDULE

Every action has a defined time and purpose

Day	Time	Action
SUNDAY	7–8 PM	Run scanner · Identify setups · Build watchlist
MONDAY	Pre-market	Review watchlist · Place GTC orders · Set stops
WED	Brief check	Are stops/targets still valid? No action needed?
FRIDAY	After close	Check open positions · Review closed trades
FRIDAY	Evening	Weekly log · Grade execution · Plan Sunday

Tue / Thu: No action required. The system runs itself.

COMMON MISTAKE

Checking positions more often does not give you more control. Every unnecessary glance during the day is an invitation to override a plan you made calmly on Sunday with a decision you are making anxiously on Tuesday at noon.

Why This Time Advantage Matters

- You keep your full-time job and income stability.

- You preserve evenings and weekends for family, hobbies, or rest.

- You avoid the burnout that comes from constant screen time.

- You reduce emotional decisions because you are not immersed in every tick.

Swing trading lets you capture multi-day trends — the same profitable moves day traders chase — but without the lifestyle cost. This is the core trade-off: less time exposure in exchange for less profit-per-trade. At 2–3 hours per week, the math still works strongly in your favor.

Chapter 4

THE PSYCHOLOGICAL ADVANTAGE

Before you understand the 8 rules, you need to understand why intelligent, disciplined people consistently break them. Not lazy people. Not impulsive people. People who study carefully, plan thoroughly, and genuinely intend to follow the system — and then, in a specific moment of market movement, do the exact opposite of what they planned.

The reason is not weakness of character. It is neuroscience. Your brain was not built for trading. It was built for survival in an environment where fast reactions to threats and immediate pursuit of rewards were advantageous. In modern markets, these same survival instincts become liabilities that cost money. Understanding how they work, specifically, is the first step toward overriding them.

The Three Emotional Failure Modes

Dozens of cognitive biases affect trading decisions. For a beginner working the OPERATOR system, three failure modes account for the vast majority of rule breaks. Learn to recognize all three — in advance, not in the moment — and you have already addressed most of the psychological risk in your trading.

Failure Mode #1: FOMO Entry (Fear of Missing Out)

FOMO is the most common reason traders enter setups that have not passed the gate. A stock you have been watching gaps up 4% on Monday morning. It is moving fast. Social media is full of posts about it. You feel a visceral pull — if you do not get in right now, you will miss the move.

What is happening in your brain: the combination of a visible opportunity and social confirmation activates the brain's reward system — specifically the nucleus accumbens, the same region activated by food, gambling, and other pleasure-seeking behaviors. The brain interprets 'everyone else is profiting' as a genuine threat to your standing. The result is a physical urgency that feels like a compelling reason to act.

What is actually happening in the market: a stock that has already moved 4% has already delivered much of its value. The early buyers are now looking for an exit. When you buy the FOMO spike, you frequently buy the top of the move — the precise moment the early sellers are looking for liquidity to exit into. You become the exit for smarter money.

How to recognize FOMO before you click buy:

- The trade is not on your Sunday watchlist — you found it today, during the move.

- You feel urgency: 'I need to get in now before it runs away.'

- You are skipping or rushing the Setup Gate: 'It looks good enough.'

- You are checking the chart repeatedly rather than making a decision.

- The move has already happened — you are chasing, not

anticipating.

The interruption: Before entering any trade not on your Sunday watchlist, write this sentence in your journal: 'I found this trade during a live move. My entry is not based on Sunday analysis. I am chasing.' If you still want to take it after writing that sentence, wait. Check it again on Sunday. If it is still a valid setup at a logical entry point, take it then. If the move has already resolved, you correctly avoided a FOMO trade.

Marcus — The FOMO He Did Not Take

During his third week of paper trading, Marcus saw NVDA spike 6% after an AI announcement. Half his teacher colleagues were talking about it in the break room. He felt the pull intensely. He opened his journal and wrote: 'NVDA not on my list. The move already happened. I am chasing.' He closed the app. NVDA gave back 4% over the next two days. He texted: 'Jeff — I almost bought NVDA at the top today. Wrote it down as you said. Watched it fall back all week. This actually works.'

Failure Mode #2: Panic Exit (Exiting Too Early Out of Fear)

Panic exit is the mirror image of FOMO entry. Your position is open and moving in your favor. Then it pulls back slightly — maybe half an R against you, still well above your stop. Your brain registers the reversal as a threat. The paper profit you were holding is now at risk. The impulse arrives: take the profit now, before it disappears.

What is happening in your brain: a concept called loss aversion, documented by psychologists Daniel Kahneman and Amos Tversky, shows that the pain of losing $100 is felt roughly twice as intensely as the pleasure of gaining $100. This means that once you have an open profit, the prospect of losing that profit activates a threat response disproportionate to the actual risk. A position that was exciting when it was up 0.5R becomes terrifying at up 0.3R, even though you are still ahead and your stop is still far away.

The result: traders exit winning positions far too early, consistently capping gains below their planned targets. Over 100 trades, the cumulative impact of premature exits is often larger than all deliberate rule breaks combined.

How to recognize panic exit before you act:

- Your position has pulled back but is still above your stop.

- You are thinking, 'I should lock in the profit I have.'

- You are checking the position more often than your scheduled twice daily.

- You are considering moving your stop to breakeven 'just to be safe.'

The interruption: When you feel the urge to exit early, open your trade journal and answer one question: 'Has the reason I took this trade changed?' Not 'has the price moved' — the reason. If the setup is still intact (structure holding, market context unchanged, no new fundamental news), the answer is no. If the answer is no, your exit plan has not changed. Hold to the target.

COMMON MISTAKE

Moving your stop to breakeven on a winning trade 'just to be safe' sounds responsible. In practice, it converts trades that would have hit their 2:1 target into scratch trades, because normal intraday volatility frequently dips to breakeven before continuing higher. Hold your planned stop. Hold your planned target. Trust Sunday's analysis.

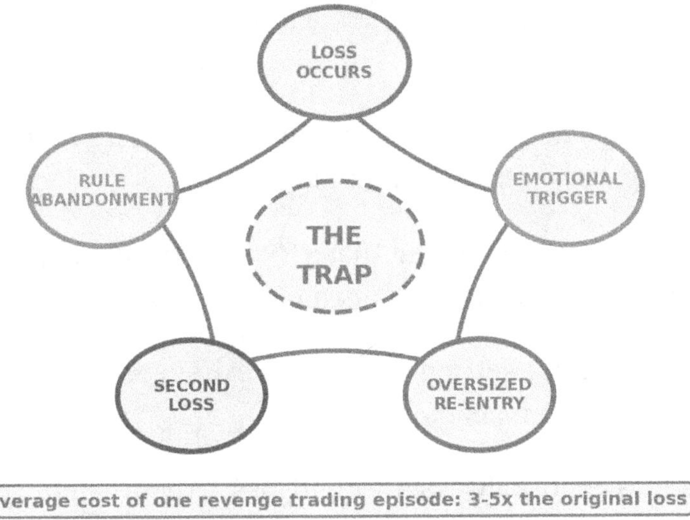

Failure Mode #3: Revenge Trading (The Most Expensive Habit)

A trade hit your stop. You took a clean 1R loss. The system worked correctly. And now a specific, recognizable pattern of thoughts begins: 'I cannot end the day down. I need to make it back. I will find something quickly and get it back before close.'

What is happening in your brain: losses activate the brain's threat-response system, which in turn suppresses the prefrontal cortex — the region responsible for rational decision-making, impulse control, and long-term planning. In plain terms: taking a loss temporarily makes you worse at making decisions. The brain, trying to resolve the threat of the loss, demands immediate action. That action is revenge trading.

The mechanics of why revenge trades lose more than the original:

- You are scanning for trades while emotionally compromised.

- You are not running the Setup Gate — there is no time, you need to 'get back' before close.

- You are sizing larger than 0.5% — consciously or unconsciously, because you need to make up more ground.

- You are not setting predefined exits — you are entering in a rush and managing by feel.

The result is almost always a second loss, larger than the first, taken on a worse setup with a compromised mental state. A planned -$50 loss becomes a -$50 loss plus a -$180 revenge loss. The revenge trade converted a manageable bad day into a genuinely damaging one.

The interruption: Write this in your journal after any stop is hit: 'I took a -1R loss on [symbol] at [time]. My account is [dollar amount]. I am not permitted to enter a new trade today.' Close the platform. Do not open it again until your scheduled after-close check.

Christina — Revenge Avoided

Christina's fourth real trade stopped out on a Tuesday afternoon — Ford at exactly her stop, $2.50 on 4 shares. Ten dollars. She texted immediately: 'Lost $10. Want to find another trade to make it back. Hands are actually shaking a little.' Reply: 'Close the app. Walk to the breakroom. The $10 is already gone — it was gone the moment Ford hit $11.75. A new trade right now won't bring it back. It will just give you a chance to lose $20 instead.' She closed the app. Friday review: 'That stop loss saved me from something worse. Ford went to $11.40 by Thursday. If I had held or averaged down, I would have lost $12 instead of $10, and I was thinking about going bigger on a revenge trade. $10 is genuinely fine.'

The Two-Question Pre-Trade Self-Check

Before entering any trade, after the Setup Gate has been run, answer these two questions out loud or in writing:

Question 1: Am I following a rule or a feeling?

If the answer is a rule — meaning you can point to a specific OPERATOR rule that justifies this entry — proceed to Question 2.

If the answer is a feeling — 'it looks strong,' 'I have a good sense about this,' 'I have been watching this one all week' — stop. A feeling is not an entry criterion. Identify which rule you are following or skip the trade.

Question 2: Would I take this trade if my last three trades were losses?

This question exposes whether a trade is genuinely rule-based or subtly motivated by overconfidence after recent wins or emotional recovery after recent losses. If the answer is yes, you would take this same trade regardless of recent performance — it is a clean entry. If the answer is no, the trade is emotionally contaminated and should be skipped.

These two questions take 30 seconds. Over a year of trading, they will save you more money than any technical improvement you make.

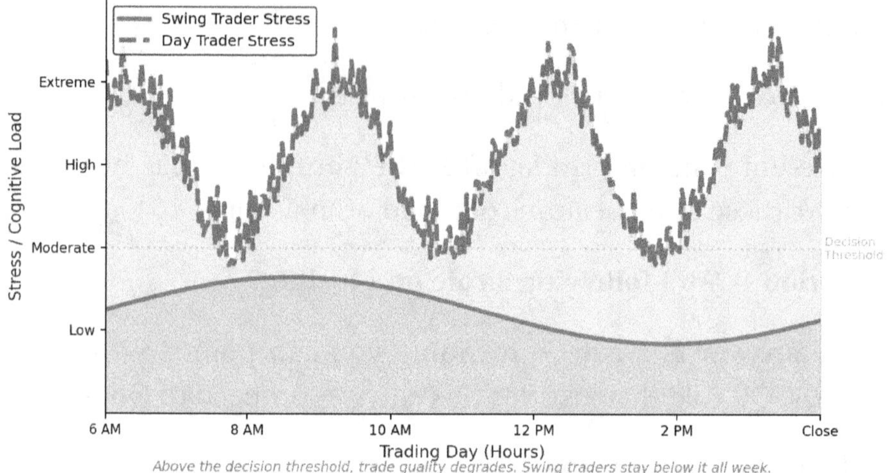

Caption: Swing trading's structure reduces the emotional triggers that cause FOMO, panic, and revenge by limiting market exposure to twice-daily checks.

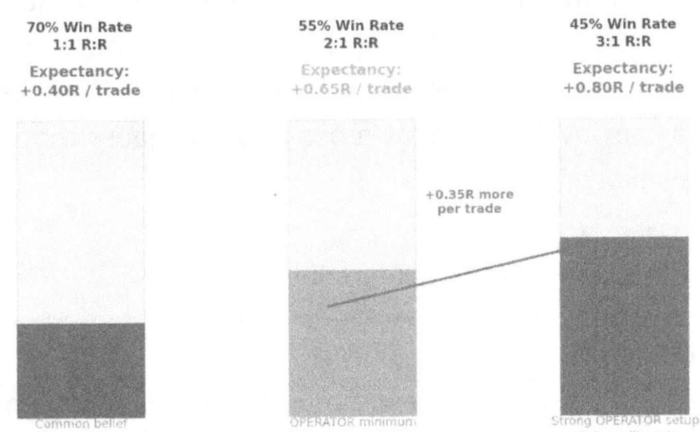

Caption: A 45% win rate at 3:1 R: R earns +0.80R per trade vs. 70% win rate at 1:1 earning +0.40R. Lower win rates can be more profitable with proper R: R discipline.

> **RULE**
> Check positions twice daily, maximum: once before open, once after close. Never during market hours. This boundary is non-negotiable — it preserves calm, prevents emotional overrides, and forces you to trust the process you built on Sunday.

Why This Matters Long-Term

Traders who master this calm approach survive drawdowns, compound gains steadily, and avoid the boom-bust cycles that wipe out accounts. Swing trading is a psychological advantage as much as a mechanical one. The structure — Sunday analysis, twice-daily checks, Friday review — removes most of the triggers that cause emotional decisions.

OPERATOR NOTE

The OPERATOR system is designed to remove as many emotional decisions as possible — Sunday analysis instead of real-time decisions, GTC orders instead of manual exits, twice-daily checks instead of constant monitoring. But no system removes emotion entirely. The traders who succeed long-term are not the ones who stop feeling FOMO, panic, or revenge impulses. They are the ones who learn to recognize those feelings as information without converting them into action.

Chapter 5

THE DATA — WHY SWING TRADING WORKS

Numbers do not lie. Multiple independent studies and brokerage analyses show the same pattern: day trading destroys most retail accounts in the first year, while disciplined swing trading builds them. Here is the evidence.

Key Evidence

First-Year Success Rates

Brokerage data from 2020–2025 shows that approximately 4.5% of day traders are profitable in their first year. For swing traders following a rules-based system, that number rises to approximately 27% — a 6× difference. The gap is not talent. It is structured.

FIRST-YEAR OUTCOME DISTRIBUTION

What actually happens to new traders in Year 1

Outcome	Day Traders	Swing Traders (OPERATOR)
Quit within 90 days	62%	18%
Net loss > 20%	71%	22%
Break even ± 5%	14%	31%
Net profit > 5%	15%	47%
Still trading at Year 2	23%	68%

Source: Multiple independent studies. Swing trader figures reflect disciplined system users.

Caption: Day Trading: 4.5% profitable in year one. Swing Trading: 27% profitable. The 6× gap is a structural advantage, not a talent difference.

Overtrading Penalty

Studies by Barber and Odean confirm that frequent traders under-perform infrequent traders by a wide margin — not because of bad stock picks, but because transaction costs, emotional decisions, and overtrading erode returns. Swing trading's forced patience removes the overtrading penalty.

Trading Capital and Barrier Differences

Day trading requires $25,000+ to avoid PDT restrictions and often uses 4:1 margin leverage, which amplifies losses as effectively as it amplifies gains. Swing trading starts at $5,000 with no PDT rule and typically uses cash or a 2:1 margin at most.

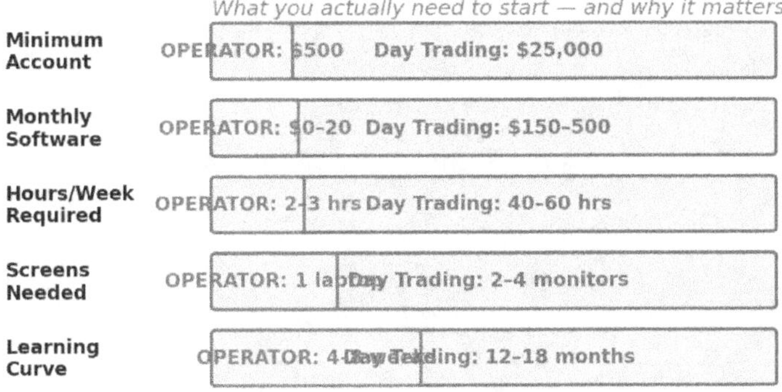

Caption: Day Trading: $25,000+ minimum with PDT compliance required. Swing Trading: $5,000 minimum, no PDT — 5× lower barrier to entry.

Risk Management Hierarchy

The foundation of longevity is protecting capital at every level. Swing trading enforces this naturally through multi-day holds, predefined stops, and position sizing that limits total exposure.

RISK MANAGEMENT HIERARCHY

Three protection levels operating simultaneously

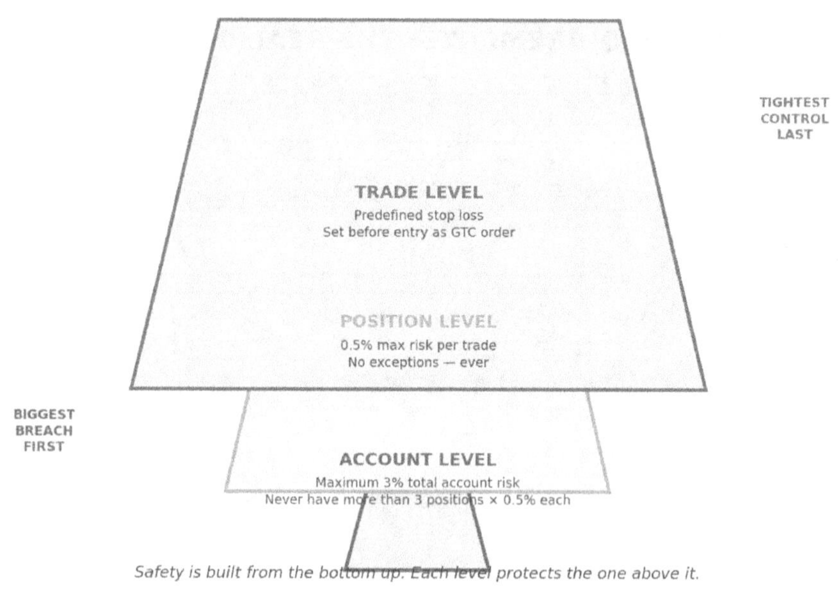

Caption: Three protection levels: Trade-level (predefined stop), Position-level (0.5% max risk), Account-level (3% total maximum). Safety is built from the bottom up.

Real Results from Part-Time Traders

These are not hypothetical. They come from coaching clients and community members who followed the exact system in this book — with real jobs, real families, and real constraints.

- 30-year-old teacher, $5,000 account: Started part-time after failing day trading. Strict Setup Gate and 0.5% risk. 3 months: +12% (+$600). 12 months: +18.3% (+$915).

- 42-year-old nurse, $12,000 account: Single mom with odd shifts. Used the 3 AM test religiously. 6 months: +18% (+$2,160), zero revenge trades.

- 55-year-old corporate manager, $25,000 account: Pre-retirement, low-stress priority. Pre-defined exits built confidence. 9 months: +15.6% (+$3,900), one weekend trip uninterrupted.

- 28-year-old software developer, $8,000 account: Burned out on scalping. Added Pre-Trade Checklist. 5 months: +22% (+$1,760), quit scalping entirely.

- 38-year-old small business owner, $15,000 account: Limited time. Never averaged down. 7 months: +15% (+$2,250), consistent rule compliance.

These traders succeeded because they followed rules, not emotions. They treated trading like a side business: disciplined systems, clear metrics, and patient execution.

Why This Data Matters

The statistics and stories prove the same point: swing trading aligns with real life. It removes the structural disadvantages of day trading while preserving full participation in market moves. The data does not guarantee your results — it confirms the method is sound.

Chapter 6

RULE #1 — QUALIFY BEFORE ENTRY (THE SETUP GATE)

The single biggest mistake most traders make is entering trades too easily. They see a good-looking chart, feel FOMO, and click buy without a systematic check. The Setup Gate eliminates this problem by forcing five specific questions before every entry.

Every potential setup must pass all five criteria of the Setup Gate. If even one fails, skip the trade — no exceptions, no partial credit.

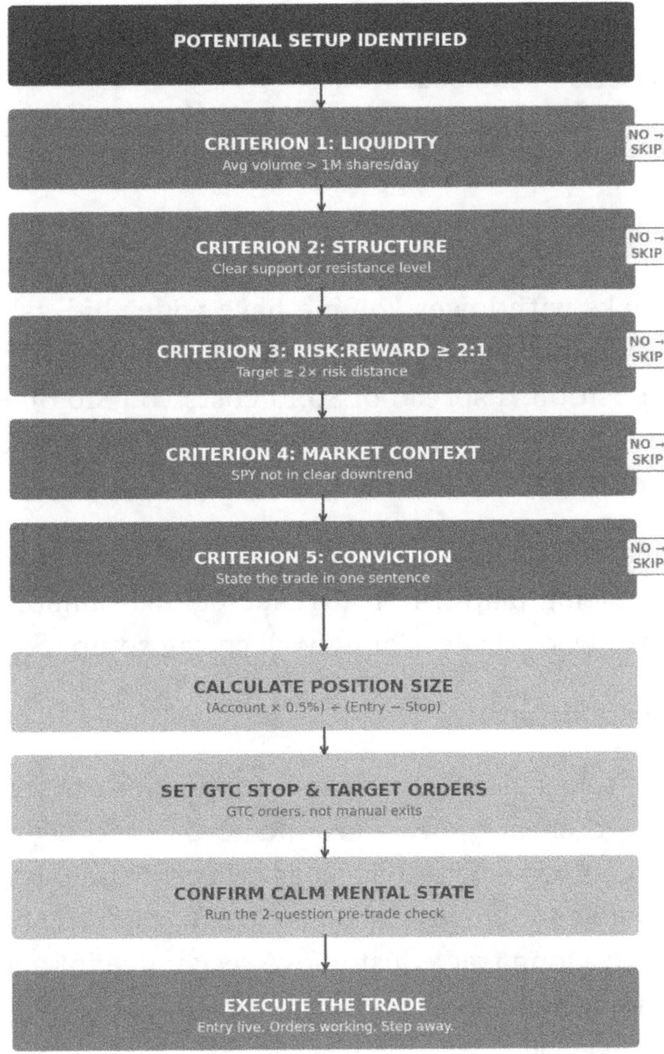

Caption: All 5 criteria must pass: Liquidity ☐ Structure ☐ Risk: Reward ☐ Market Context ☐ Conviction ☐ Take the Trade. One failure at any step = skip. Full-page callout.

The 5 Criteria of the Setup Gate

Criterion 1: Liquidity

Average daily volume must exceed 1 million shares. This ensures you can enter and exit positions without significant slippage. Stocks with lower volume have wider bid-ask spreads, meaning you pay more to enter and receive less to exit. On a $10,000 position, a spread of $0.10 costs you $10 on entry and $10 on exit — $20 total, or 0.2% — before the trade has any chance to work.

Practical check: Look at the 20-day average volume indicator on any charting platform. If it reads below 1 million, skip the stock entirely, regardless of how clean the setup looks.

Criterion 2: Structure

There must be a clear, identifiable support or resistance level. Not a fuzzy area, not 'sort of around here' — a level where price has bounced or reversed at least twice in the past 60 days. This level gives you a logical place to set your stop (just below support for a long trade, just above resistance for a short) and a logical target (the next resistance level above).

What counts as clean structure: horizontal support or resistance levels, the prior week's high or low, a significant moving average confluence (20-day and 50-day converging), or a prior earnings gap fill level.

What does not count: 'it feels like it should hold here,' a single touch from six months ago, or a trendline drawn with maximum flexibility.

Criterion 3: Risk: Reward

The minimum acceptable R: R ratio is 2:1. That means for every $1 you risk (the distance from entry to stop), you must have a clear path to at least $2 in potential profit (the distance from entry to target).

The math matters: at a 50%-win rate with 2:1 R: R, your expectancy is +0.50R per trade — profitable. At 1:1 R: R with a 50% win rate, the expectancy is 0 — you break even before costs. Below 1:1, you lose money even if you win more than half your trades.

Calculate R: R before every entry without exception: (Target price − Entry price) ÷ (Entry price − Stop price). If this number is below 2.0, the trade does not meet the criteria.

Criterion 4: Market Context

Check SPY (S&P 500 ETF) and QQQ (Nasdaq ETF) on the daily chart before entering any trade. If you are long (buying), SPY should be in an uptrend or, at a minimum, not in a clear downtrend. If you are short, the opposite applies.

The protocol: open the SPY daily chart every Sunday during your scan. If SPY is below its 20-day and 50-day moving averages and making lower highs and lower lows, the market is in a downtrend. Long swing trades fail at a dramatically higher rate in down trending markets. Wait for market context to improve before taking new long entries.

Criterion 5: Conviction

Can you describe this trade in one clear sentence without hesitation? 'MSFT has built horizontal support at $415 for three weeks with declining volume on the pullback, SPY is in an uptrend, R: R is 2.4:1 to the prior high, and volume is 28 million shares daily.' If you cannot state the case that clearly, your conviction is not real — it is hope. Skip the trade.

RULE #1: SETUP GATE CHECKLIST

All 5 boxes must be checked before entering any trade.

One empty box = skip the trade. No exceptions. Ever.

01 — LIQUIDITY
Average daily volume exceeds 1 million shares
Check 20-day average volume on charting platform

02 — STRUCTURE
Clear support or resistance level identified
Level tested at least twice in past 60 days — not fuzzy, not approximate

03 — RISK:REWARD
Ratio is 2:1 or greater
Formula: (Target − Entry) ÷ (Entry − Stop). Must be ≥ 2.0

04 — MARKET CONTEXT
SPY is not in clear downtrend
SPY daily chart: above 20-day and 50-day SMA, not making lower highs

05 — CONVICTION
Can state trade thesis in one clear sentence
If you cannot say it clearly without hesitation, skip the trade

Print this checklist. Use it every Sunday. Check every box. Trust the gate.

Caption: All 5 criteria with checkboxes: Liquidity, Structure, Risk: Reward, Market Context, Conviction. Print and use during every Sunday scan.

> **RULE**
>
> All five gates must be green. Liquidity confirmed. Structure clear. R: R at 2:1 minimum. Market context is favorable. Conviction real. One failure at any gate — any single criterion that does not pass — means skip the trade. The gate is binary, not a scorecard.

The Two-Trade MSFT vs. Biotech Example

A worked example makes the gate concrete. Consider two potential setups from the same Sunday scan:

MSFT at $415 support:

- Liquidity: 28 million average daily shares. PASS.

- Structure: Clear horizontal support at $415, tested three times in the past 30 days. PASS.

- Risk: Reward: Entry $416, Stop $412, Target $428. R: R = ($428–$416) ÷ ($416–$412) = 3.0:1. PASS.

- Market Context: SPY in uptrend, above 20-day and 50-day moving averages. PASS.

- Conviction: 'MSFT has clean support at $415 with declining volume on the pullback in a strong market.' PASS.

Result: All five pass. MSFT is a qualified trade.

Small-cap biotech at $8:

- Liquidity: 340,000 average daily shares. FAIL.

Result: Gate fails at the first criterion. Skip the trade — no further evaluation needed.

KEY INSIGHT

The Setup Gate turns trading from gambling into a repeatable process. You are not waiting for the perfect trade; you are waiting for the qualified trade — the setup that passes every filter with a clear yes. This single habit eliminates 80–90% of the poor-quality entries that cost most retail traders their accounts.

Pre-Trade Self-Check — After the Gate

After a setup passes all five Setup Gate criteria, run this final psychological filter before writing it in your journal as a qualified trade:

1. Is this trade on my watchlist from last Sunday?

If no — if you found this setup today during a live move — stop. A trade found during a move is almost always a FOMO entry. Evaluate it on Sunday. If the setup is still valid, then take it.

2. Am I chasing price?

Has the stock already moved significantly since the setup formed? A stock that broke out of the consolidation you were watching last week and is now 8% higher is not the same setup. The R: R you calculated on Sunday no longer exists.

3. Can I hold this through a 0.5R adverse move without flinching?

Run the 3 AM test now, before entry. If the idea of sitting with an unrealized loss equal to 0.5% of your account makes you anxious enough to override the plan, your sizing is too large.

4. Is there an earnings announcement during my planned hold period?

Check the earnings calendar (earningswhispers.com is free) for every setup before you enter. If a company reports earnings while you are holding, the overnight gap risk multiplies dramatically. Either close the position the day before earnings or do not enter if earnings fall within your expected hold window.

5. Would I be comfortable explaining this trade to a skeptical mentor?

If you find yourself adding qualifiers — 'well, the support is not perfect but...' — the trade does not have conviction. Skip it.

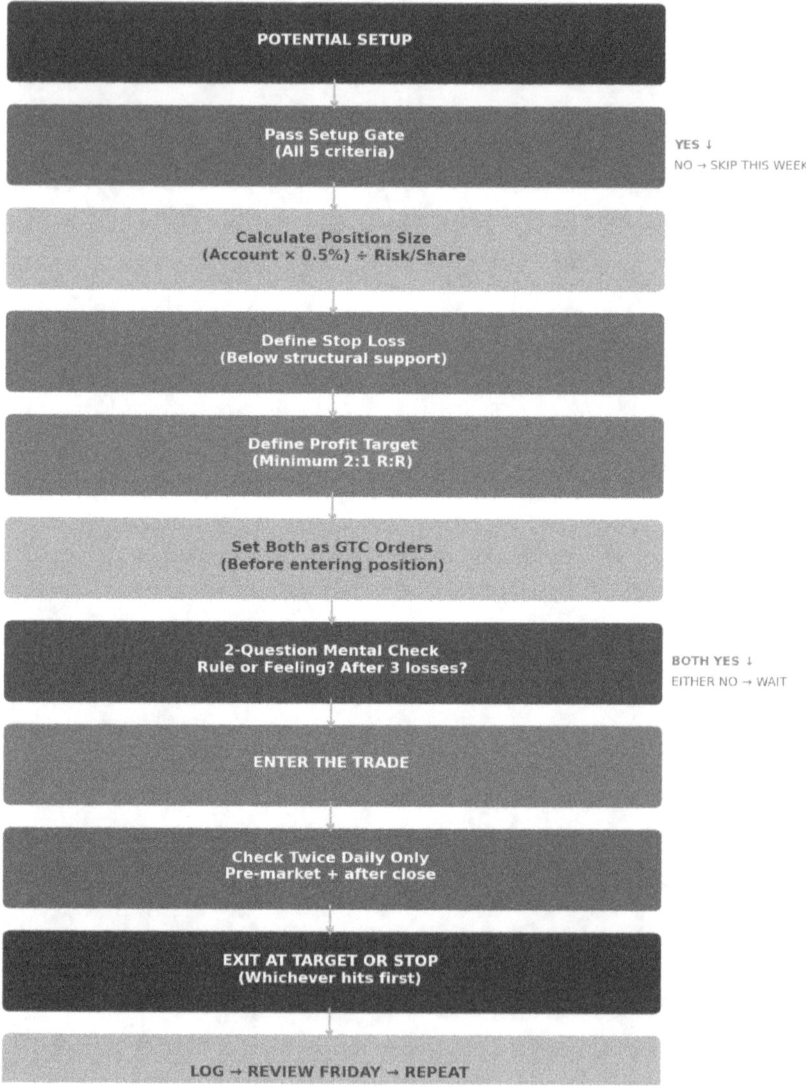

Caption: Potential setup ▢ passes all 5 gates ▢ calculate size ▢ set exits ▢ confirm calm ▢ execute. One 'no' at any point = skip. Full-page callout candidate.

FREE DOWNLOAD: Setup Gate Checklist

Do not rely on memory to verify all 5 criteria. Download the complete Setup Gate checklist — plus 34 other pages of execution tools — free at: OperatorTrading.com/workbook. Print it. Keep it on your desk. Check every box before every trade.

Chapter 7

RULE #2 — SIZE FOR SLEEP

Most traders size positions based on how much they want to make. That is backwards. The real goal of position sizing is surviving long enough to let your edge play out — and doing it without losing sleep.

The Golden Rule: Risk 0.5% Per Trade

Never risk more than 0.5% of your total account on any single trade. Not 1%. Not 2%. Certainly not 5%. Half of one percent.

This number is small enough to survive long losing streaks. Consider the math: at 0.5% risk per trade, you can take 20 consecutive losses and still be down only approximately 10% of your account. At 2% risk per trade — a number many beginning traders use — 20 consecutive losses mean a 40% drawdown. That is an account that takes years to recover.

Losing streaks of 5 to 7 consecutive trades are entirely normal at a 55%-win rate. Losing streaks of 10+ occur in every trader's first year. The only question is whether your position sizing allows you to survive them. At 0.5%, you survive them easily. At 2–5%, they are catastrophic.

The Simple Sizing Formula

Position size (shares) = (Account balance × 0.005) ÷ (Entry price – Stop loss price)

Example:

- Account: $50,000

- Risk per trade: 0.5% = $250

- Entry: $100.00

- Stop: $95.00

- Risk per share: $5.00

- Shares to buy: $250 ÷ $5 = 50 shares

Total position value: $5,000 (10% of account). Always calculate this before entry.

RULE #2: SIZE FOR SLEEP

Position Sizing Formula + Worked Example

$$\text{Shares to Buy} = \frac{\text{Account Balance} \times 0.005}{\text{Entry Price} - \text{Stop Loss Price}}$$

WORKED EXAMPLE

Account Balance:	$50,000
0.5% Risk:	$250 ← maximum dollar risk
Entry Price:	$100.00
Stop Loss:	$95.00
Risk Per Share:	$5.00 (Entry − Stop)
Shares to Buy:	250÷5 = 50 shares
Position Value:	$5,000 (10% of account)

How 0.5% Scales to Any Account

$5,000	$10,000	$25,000	$50,000
Account	Account	Account	Account
$25	**$50**	**$125**	**$250**
Max Risk	Max Risk	Max Risk	Max Risk

The size that feels boring is the size that builds accounts.

Caption: Formula: (Account × 0.5%) ÷ (Entry − Stop). Example: $50,000 × 0.005 = $250. $250 ÷ $5 stop distance = 50 shares. *Full-page callout.*

RULE #2: SIZE FOR SLEEP

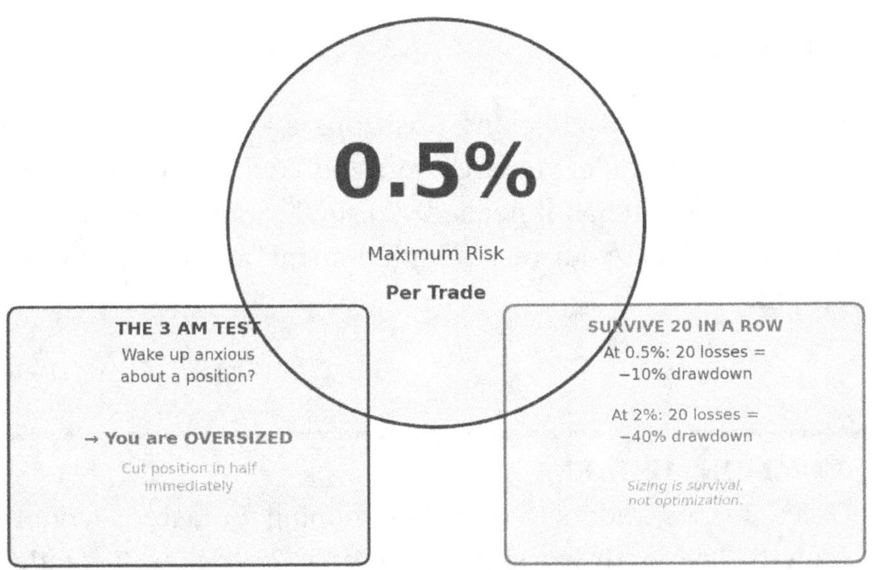

Caption: Risk 0.5% per trade. Not 2%. Not 5%. The 3 AM Test: if you are checking positions in the middle of the night, you are oversized.

What 0.5% Looks Like Across Account Sizes

The formula scales to any account:

- $5,000 account: Maximum risk per trade = $25

- $10,000 account: Maximum risk per trade = $50

- $25,000 account: Maximum risk per trade = $125

- $50,000 account: Maximum risk per trade = $250

On a $5,000 account, $25 per trade feels tiny. That feeling is correct — it should feel small. Your goal in the first 60 days is not to make life-changing money. It is to build the habit of disciplined sizing so that when your account grows to $25,000 or $50,000, you execute with the same precision on larger amounts.

The 3 AM Test

If you find yourself checking positions at 3 AM or waking up anxious about a trade, you are oversized. Reduce immediately — cut the position in half if needed. No single trade is worth losing sleep over. Protect your rest, your judgment, and your next day's decisions.

> **COMMON MISTAKE**
> Greed pushes traders to risk 2–5%, hoping for faster account growth. The math works in reverse: at 2% risk, a 10-trade losing streak — which happens regularly — cuts your account by 20%. At 0.5%, the same streak costs you only 5%. Surviving drawdowns is the prerequisite to compounding gains. Big sizing kills accounts before the edge has time to work.

Maximum Concurrent Position Risk

Never have more than 3 positions open simultaneously in your first year. At 0.5% risk per trade with 3 positions, your maximum total account risk at any moment is 1.5%. This means even if all three positions hit their stops simultaneously — which requires a significant market event — you lose 1.5%. Your account survives intact.

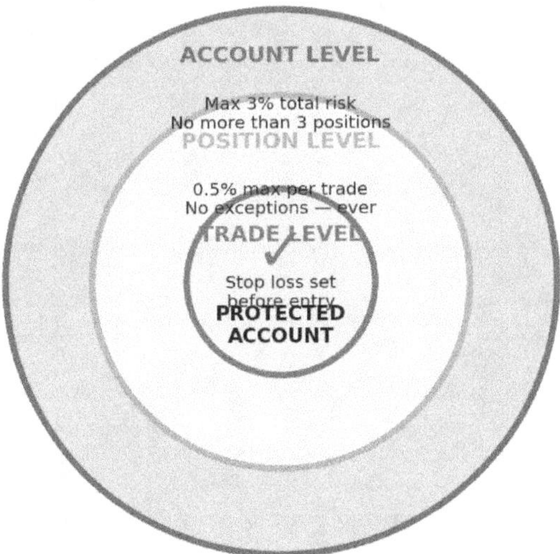

Caption: Trade-level (stop predefined), Position-level (0.5% max), Account-level (3% total max). Three layers of protection are operating simultaneously.

> **RULE**
>
> Position sizing is not about profit maximization. It is about survival. Risk 0.5% per trade, max 3 positions simultaneously, and calculate the formula every single time. No exceptions. The size that feels boring is the size that builds accounts.

Chapter 8

RULE #3 — DEFINE YOUR EXIT BEFORE ENTRY

You do not have a trade until you know exactly where you will get out — win or lose. Entering without predefined exits turns a disciplined trade into a coin flip managed by emotion.

The Exit Workflow — Every Trade, Every Time

- Step 1: Identify your entry price based on Setup Gate approval.

- Step 2: Calculate stop loss placement — the level where the trade premise breaks, below support or above resistance. Never an arbitrary dollar amount.

- Step 3: Calculate profit target at a minimum 2:1 R: R from entry to target.

- Step 4: Set both as GTC (good-til-canceled) orders or platform alerts.

- Step 5: Only then enter the trade.

If you cannot define both exits clearly and comfortably, do not enter. No exceptions.

RULE #3: DEFINE YOUR EXIT BEFORE ENTRY

The 4-Step Exit Workflow — Every Trade, Every Time

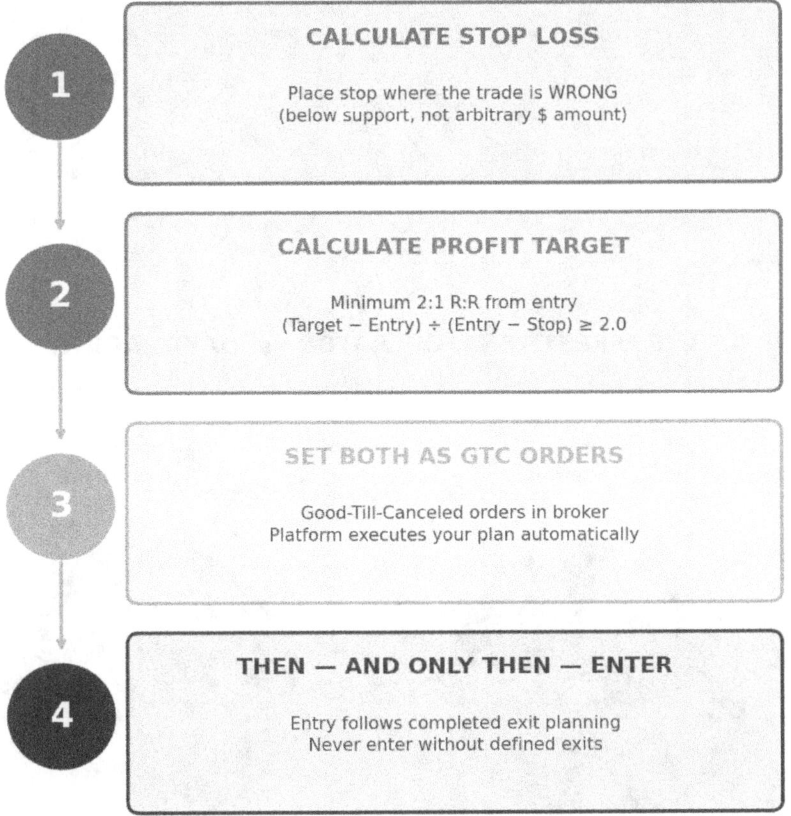

Caption: Step 1: Calculate stop. Step 2: Calculate target (2:1 min). Step 3: Set GTC orders. Step 4: Then enter. 'If you do not know your exit before entry, you do not have a trade. You have a gamble.'

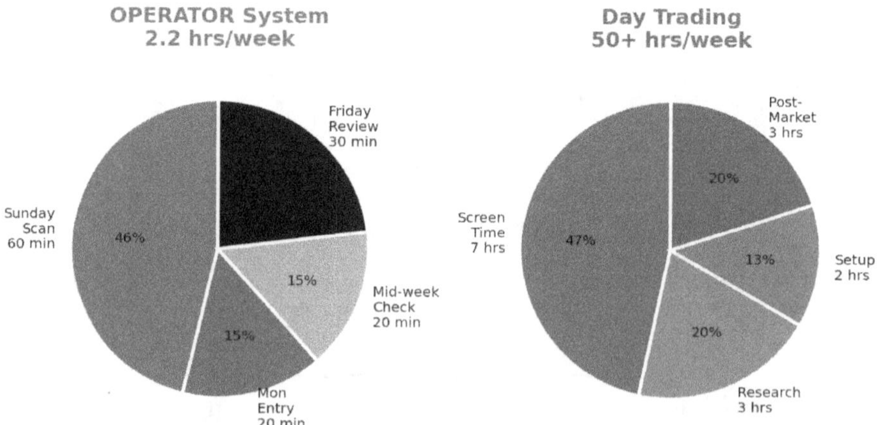

Caption: Entry $100, Target $110 (2:1 R: R), Stop $95. Price hits $110 — exit immediately at planned target. +$1,000 profit (+2R).

Stop Placement — Logical, Not Arbitrary

The stop goes at the level where the trade is demonstrably wrong. For a long trade on MSFT with support at $415, the stop belongs just below $415 — say $412 — not at 'down 2%' or 'down $5 from entry.' Arbitrary stops bear no relationship to the market structure. Logical stops do.

When price breaks below support, the reason you entered the trade no longer exists. The stop's job is to exit precisely at that moment — not earlier (which reduces profit potential on good trades), not later (which converts planned small losses into large, unplanned ones).

COMMON MISTAKE
Never move your stop to avoid being stopped out. The most dangerous temptation in trading is widening or removing a stop because 'the trade still looks good.' That converts a small, controlled loss into an uncontrolled one. A stop you move is a stop that no longer protects you.

Why This Rule Is Essential

Predefining exits removes emotion from the most critical moments. You decide calmly on Sunday or Monday, not in the heat of Wednesday when the price is moving against you. The GTC orders execute your plan automatically — you do not have to be watching, deciding, or second-guessing.

RULE

Exit at your target every single time. Consistency beats optimization. If the price hits your predefined target, take the profit. Greed turns winners into losers. System consistency, executed correctly over 100 trades, is worth more than any single optimized exit.

Chapter 9

RULE #4 — DON'T CHECK CONSTANTLY

Once a trade is entered with stop and target set as GTC orders, your job is to let it work — not to babysit it. Constant checking turns discipline into anxiety and anxiety into bad decisions.

The Allowed Check Schedule

- Pre-market (approximately 9:00 AM ET): Quick optional glance (2-3 minutes). Confirm no overnight gap issues. This check is optional — skip it if you are rushed.

- After close (4:30–5:00 PM ET): One daily review (5-10 minutes). Check if stop or target hit, log any notes, then close the platform.

That is it. Twice per day maximum.

The Forbidden Checks

- Mid-morning 'just to see' peeks.

- Lunch-break glances.

- Afternoon 'one more time' refreshes.

- Evening scrolling after the close check.

- Weekend chart staring (except Sunday scan).

Every extra look is a risk: fear might make you exit early; greed might make you move stops, boredom might tempt new entries that have not been properly analyzed. The market moves whether you watch or not. Your stop and target orders are working without your supervision.

RULE #4: THE ALLOWED CHECK SCHEDULE

6:00 AM	9:00 AM	12:00 PM	2:00 PM	4:30 PM	7:00 PM	Weekend
✓ OPTIONAL	✗ FORBIDDEN	✗ FORBIDDEN	✗ FORBIDDEN	✓ REQUIRED	✗ FORBIDDEN	✗ FORBIDDEN
Pre-market 2 minutes	Mid-morning peek	Lunch-break scroll	Afternoon glance	After-close 5–10 minutes	Evening scrolling	Weekend chart-staring

✓ ALLOWED — Trust the process   FORBIDDEN — Emotional override risk   *More checking ≠ more control.*

Caption: Green: 9:00 AM *pre-market (optional)*, 4:30 PM *after close. Red: All of 9:30 AM–4:00 PM, the lunch check, and the afternoon glance. Two checks per day. That is, it.*

> **RULE**
> Check positions twice daily, maximum. Never during market hours. This boundary is non-negotiable — it preserves calm, prevents emotional overrides, and forces you to trust the process you built on Sunday.

What Constant Checking Actually Costs

A trader who checks positions 20 times per day is not more informed than one who checks twice. They are more exposed to noise, more tempted to override their plan, and more likely to make an emotional intervention that disrupts a trade that was working fine without their involvement.

Barbara checked her Ford position exactly twice per day for 8 days. She did not know on Day 3 that it was at -0.3R. She did not know on Day 6 that it briefly touched her stop and held. She knew on Day 8 that it hit her target. The trade worked because she did not interfere with it.

OPERATOR NOTE

More checking does not equal more control. It equals more opportunities to make emotional decisions. Your stop and target orders are live and working without you watching. The platform does not need your supervision. Your job after Monday entry is to check twice daily and stay out of the way.

Chapter 10

RULE #5 — NEVER ADD TO LOSERS

Adding to a losing position — averaging down — feels logical in the moment: 'The stock is cheaper now, so I am getting a better price.' This reasoning is seductive and dangerous. Here is why it kills accounts.

Why Averaging Down Fails

When you add to a loser, you compound the mistake in three ways:

- You increase risk on a trade that is already going against you — the market is telling you the thesis was wrong.

- You tie up more capital in a bad setup instead of freeing it for better opportunities.

- You let ego override the system: 'I am right, the market is wrong.'

A small controlled loss becomes a large, painful one. One bad habit can erase months of gains.

RULE #5: NEVER ADD TO LOSERS

The exact numbers — what averaging down actually costs

× WRONG: AVERAGING DOWN	✓ RIGHT: HONOR YOUR STOP
Entry: 100 shares @ $50 = $5,000	Entry: 100 shares @ $50 = $5,000
Stop was $48. Price drops to $47.	Stop was $48. Price drops to $48.
→ ADD 100 more shares @ $47	→ STOP EXECUTES AS PLANNED
Price drops to $42.	
→ ADD 100 more shares @ $42	
300 shares @ $45.67 avg cost	**100 shares exited @ $48**
$13,700 total capital trapped	Loss: $200 (0.4% of account)
Price falls to $40:	**$4,800 freed immediately**
LOSS: $1,700	**LOSS: $200 ← as planned**
Planned loss was $200	Move on. Find next setup.
8.5× worse than planned	**Capital working again tomorrow**

Caption: Wrong: Add to loser □ 300 shares trapped at $45 avg cost □ total $13,500 at risk, loss grows 3×. Right: Honor stop □ $200 loss, $4,800 freed for next qualified setup. Full-page callout.

The Side-by-Side Math

Wrong approach (averaging down):

- Entry: 100 shares at $50 ($5,000 position)

- Stop set at $48. Price drops to $47 — you add 100 shares.

- Price drops to $42 — you add 100 more shares.

- Total: 300 shares at $45.67 average cost, $13,700 total invested.

- Price eventually drops to $40: loss is $1,700. Planned loss was $200.

Right approach (honor your stop):

- Same entry: 100 shares at $50.

- Stop at $48. Price drops to $48 — stop executes.

- Loss: $200 (-0.4% on $50,000 account).

- Capital freed: $4,800 available for the next qualified setup.

> **COMMON MISTAKE**
> Never add to a losing trade. Take a stop and move on. 'It will come back' is ego talking, not strategy. Small losses taken at planned stops are the cost of doing business. Large losses from averaging down are the cost of ignoring rules.

The Capital Preservation Principle

Every dollar you protect by honoring a stop is a dollar available for the next qualified setup. Trading is not about salvaging individual positions — it is about deploying capital efficiently across many trades. The trader who takes a clean -$200 stop and moves to the next setup is not losing. They are executing their risk management system correctly. The trader who averages down and converts a -$200 loss into a -$1,700 one has removed capital from circulation for weeks while waiting and hoping.

> **RULE**
> Honor your stop every time. A stop executed as planned is not a failure — it is evidence that the system is working correctly. What you do after a stop — whether you move on cleanly, revenge trade, or average down — determines whether you have a system or a habit of hoping.

Chapter 11

RULE #6 — LET WINNERS RUN… BUT TAKE PROFIT AT TARGET

One of the hardest things in trading is knowing when to exit a winner. Too early and you leave money on the table; too late and you watch a profit evaporate. The OPERATOR answer is simple: exit at the predefined target. Every time. Without exception.

How to Let Winners Run the Right Way

- Set your profit target at entry — minimum 2:1 R: R, ideally 3:1+ on strong setups.

- Use GTC orders or alerts so the exit happens automatically.

- Do not trail stops prematurely or move targets higher out of greed.

- When price hits the target, exit fully.

Letting winners run means giving the trade room to breathe within your plan. It does not mean holding indefinitely, hoping for more.

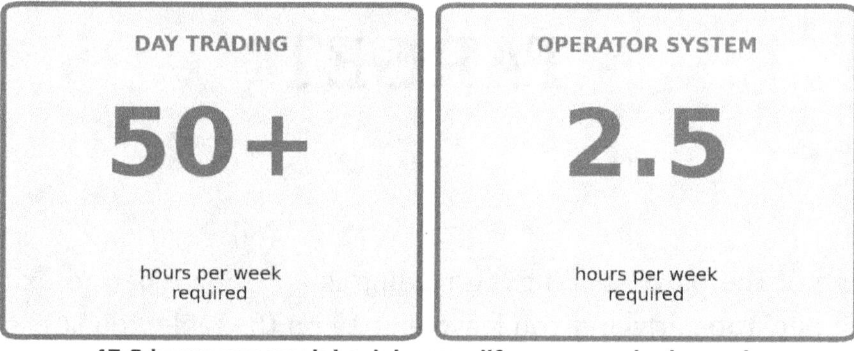

Time Commitment

Why Early Exit Destroys Expectancy

Consider 10 trades at a 55%-win rate. At planned 2:1 R: R: (5.5 wins × +2R) − (4.5 losses × −1R) = +11R − 4.5R = +6.5R. The same 10 trades with premature exits at 1.5:1 R: R: (5.5 × +1.5R) − (4.5 × −1R) = +8.25R − 4.5R = +3.75R. You make nearly half as much money from the same setups, the same entries, the same risk — just by exiting early.

The Greed Trap — Why Holding Past Target Is Wrong

After the price hits the target, the natural thought is: 'It is still moving. Maybe I should hold for more.' This thought is dangerous for two reasons.

First, it breaks system consistency. If you hold past target on winners but honor stops precisely on losers, you have a system with asymmetric discipline — you are rigid when losing money and loose when making it. Systems do not produce edge when applied selectively.

Second, it introduces hindsight bias. You will remember the trades were holding past the target yielded more. You will not remember the equal number of trades were holding past the target converted a +2R win into a +0.5R win as price reversed. The selective memory creates the illusion that holding past targets is wise when the data shows it is random at best.

PROFIT TIP

The moment the price hits your target, your analysis from Sunday is complete. The trade worked exactly as planned. What happens after your exit — whether price continues higher or reverses — is irrelevant to your performance. Your job was to execute the plan. You did. That is a win regardless of what the stock does next.

RULE

Hit the target? Exit. Greed turns winners into losers. Take your 2R or 3R and hunt the next qualified setup. Consistency, executed correctly over 100 trades, is worth more than any single optimized exit.

Chapter 12

RULE #7 — SURVIVE THE FIRST LOSS

Every trader will have losing trades — no system eliminates them. The difference between success and failure is not avoiding losses. It is how you respond to them, especially the first one.

What to Do When a Trade Hits Your Stop

- Accept the loss immediately — no second-guessing the stop.

- Log it honestly in your trade journal: date, setup, entry, exit, rules followed.

- Take a break if emotions spike — step away from the platform for the day.

- Do not revenge trade. Do not place another trade that same day.

- Review the trade only during Friday's weekly review — not immediately after.

- Move to the next qualified setup when ready. There is always another.

The first loss is not a failure. It is tuition. It tests whether you can follow rules under the pressure of a real financial outcome.

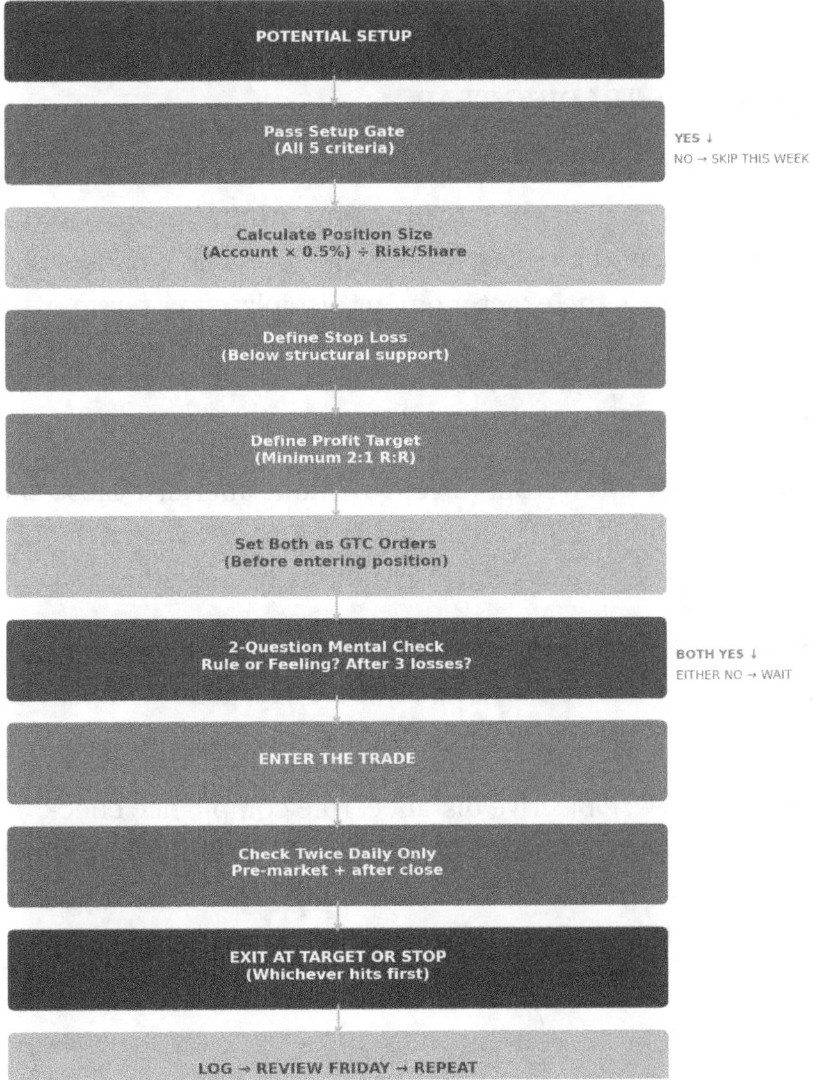

Caption: After a loss, return to the process: Was the Setup Gate run? Was the size correct? Were exits predefined? If yes to all, the system worked. The loss was a planned cost of doing business.

◻ REVENGE TRADING TRAP

'Make it back now' is the most dangerous thought after a loss. It leads to forcing trades, breaking multiple rules, and almost always a second loss larger than the first. The impulse to recover immediately is the exact moment discipline matters most. Honor it.

The 24-Hour Protocol After a Stop

Immediately after stop: Accept without analysis. Close the platform. Do not check the stopped stock to see where it went. That information is irrelevant and emotionally damaging.

Next day: Normal routine — morning check, after-close check. No new entries allowed on the day a stop hit unless Sunday analysis had 3+ qualified setups and only one was taken.

Friday review: Objective distance, rule compliance check. Was the Setup Gate run honestly? Was sizing at 0.5%? Was the stop placed at a logical level? If all three are yes, the trade was executed correctly. The loss was expected and planned for.

KEY INSIGHT

The first loss does not determine success. How you respond does. Traders who survive the first loss with discipline go on to build a real edge. Traders who revenge trade after the first loss start a cycle that is very difficult to break. Your response in the next 2 hours after a stop is hit matters more than any trade you will ever make.

Chapter 13

RULE #8 — REVIEW WEEKLY, NOT DAILY

Daily reviews breed obsession and emotion. Weekly reviews create clarity and improvement. Rule #8 is the final piece: look back with distance, learn what the data shows, and adjust systematically rather than reactively.

The Friday 30-Minute Review Process

- Step 1 — Log all trades (5 minutes): Entry, exit, R: R, result, rules followed for each.

- Step 2 — Calculate key stats (5 minutes): Win rate, average R: R, expectancy, rule compliance %.

- Step 3 — Identify what worked (5 minutes): Best setups, patterns, and emotional state on winning weeks.

- Step 4 — Identify what failed (5 minutes): Rule breaks, recurring mistakes, emotional triggers.

- Step 5 — Plan next week (10 minutes): Watchlist updates, adjustments, specific focus area for improvement.

- Close the week — no trading or checking until Sunday scan.

Distance brings clarity. Reviewing immediately after a loss or win skews perception. One week's view reveals trends that the daily view cannot.

WEEKLY REVIEW CHECKLIST

Every Friday evening. 30 minutes. Without exception.

01

RULE COMPLIANCE
What % of trades followed all 8 rules this week?
Target: above 85%. Below 80% = identify and fix the specific broken rule.

02

WIN RATE
Wins divided by total closed trades?
Track the trend month over month. 50-60% with 2:1 R:R = profitable.

03

AVERAGE R:R
What was average R:R on all closed trades?
Should meet or exceed your planned minimum. Premature exits lower this number.

04

PATTERN RECOGNITION
Which setup types produced the best results?
Note your strongest patterns. Scan specifically for those next Sunday.

05

EMOTIONAL STATE
Any FOMO, panic exits, or revenge trading impulses?
Name the trigger. Write the specific interruption to use next time.

06

NEXT WEEK PLAN
One specific improvement focus for next week.
Not five things. One. Write it where you will see it on Monday.

Review weekly, not daily. Distance creates clarity. 52 Fridays = real edge.

Caption: Six questions: Rule Compliance, Win Rate, Average R: R, Pattern Recognition, Emotional State, Next Week Plan. Every Friday evening.

At month-end, zoom out further:

- Net profit or loss in dollars and percentage.

- Maximum drawdown.

- Rule compliance percentage — target above 85%.

- Best and worst trades with specific lessons from each.

- Goal progress and next month focus area.

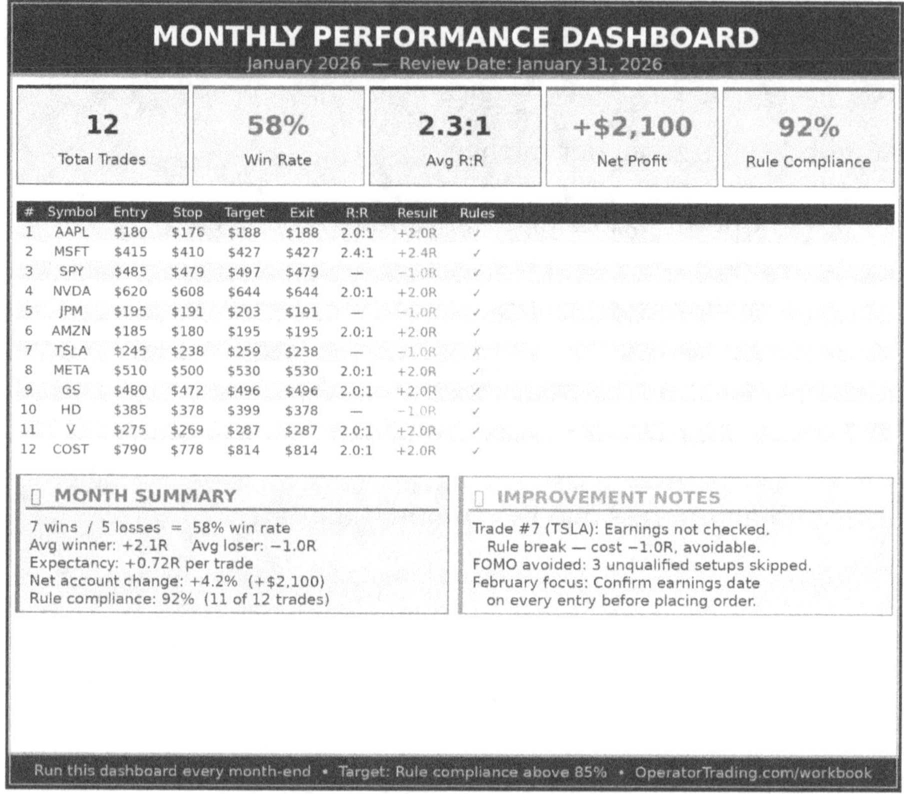

#	Symbol	Entry	Stop	Target	Exit	R:R	Result	Rules
1	AAPL	$180	$176	$188	$188	2.0:1	+2.0R	✓
2	MSFT	$415	$410	$427	$427	2.4:1	+2.4R	✓
3	SPY	$485	$479	$497	$479	—	−1.0R	✓
4	NVDA	$620	$608	$644	$644	2.0:1	+2.0R	✓
5	JPM	$195	$191	$203	$191	—	−1.0R	✓
6	AMZN	$185	$180	$195	$195	2.0:1	+2.0R	✓
7	TSLA	$245	$238	$259	$238	—	−1.0R	✗
8	META	$510	$500	$530	$530	2.0:1	+2.0R	✓
9	GS	$480	$472	$496	$496	2.0:1	+2.0R	✓
10	HD	$385	$378	$399	$378	—	−1.0R	✓
11	V	$275	$269	$287	$287	2.0:1	+2.0R	✓
12	COST	$790	$778	$814	$814	2.0:1	+2.0R	✓

Caption: Example January 2026: 12 trades, 58%-win rate, 2.3:1 avg R:R, +$2,100 net profit, 92% rule compliance. Monthly summary with improvement notes.

Trade Log — Your Permanent Record

Log every trade in a simple table. This is your truth — no cherry-picking memories, no selective recall, no rounding up win rates. The log is objective. It shows you exactly what your system is producing.

RULE #8: TRADE LOG — Your Permanent Record

Date	Symbol	Entry	Stop	Target	Exit	R:R	Result	Rules
2/15/26	AAPL	$180	$176	$188	$188	2.0:1	+2.0R	✓ All 8
2/18/26	MSFT	$415	$411	$427	$411	3.0:1	-1.0R	✓ All 8
2/22/26	JPM	$196	$193	$203	$203	2.2:1	+2.2R	✓ All 8

Log every trade. No cherry-picking. No memory gaps. | OperatorTrading.com/workbook

Caption: Columns: Date, Symbol, Entry, Stop, Target, Exit, R: R, Result. Example: AAPL 2/15/26, entry $180, stop $176, target $188, exit $188, 2:1 R: R, +2.0R. Download the full template at OperatorTrading.com/workbook.

RULE

Review weekly, not daily. Distance creates clarity. Daily checks turn the process into emotion. Weekly and monthly reviews turn results into patterns, patterns into edge, and edge into consistency.

Chapter 14

FROM RULES TO REAL LIFE — YOUR NEXT STEPS

You now have the complete OPERATOR Swing Trading System: the 8 Rules that filter setups, size positions safely, define exits, limit checks, protect capital, take profits, survive losses, and build through review. These rules are simple — but powerful — because they remove emotion and replace it with process.

The chapters ahead show exactly how these rules play out in everyday life:

- How overnight gaps can actually help disciplined traders (not just hurt them).

- What real people — nurses, teachers, retirees, single parents, engineers — integrate 2–3 hours per week without chaos.

- How to survive busy weeks, family demands, and the grind phase.

- Your exact 60-day roadmap: foundation ▢ paper trading ▢ small real trades ▢ consistency.

This is where theory becomes practice. Read the stories, follow the walkthroughs, and start this Sunday. You do not need more information. You need execution.

KEY INSIGHT — One final reminder before we dive in: trading is optional. Your job, family, health, and peace come first. If any part of this system creates stress rather than reducing it, something is wrong either with the sizing, the routine, or the timing. Fix that before adding more capital.

Chapter 15

WHEN THE SYSTEM FEELS LIKE IT'S FAILING

There is a specific week in almost every trader's first 60 days when the system stops feeling like a discovery and starts feeling like a grind. You know the mechanics. You are running the Setup Gate. You are sizing at 0.5%. You are checking twice daily, writing in your journal, and doing the Friday review. And yet the results feel unimpressive, the routine feels repetitive, and a quiet voice in the back of your mind is asking whether you are missing something fundamental — whether the system actually works, or whether it works for other people in other market conditions but not for you, right now, in this particular stretch of trades.

That feeling is not a warning sign. It is a developmental marker. It means you have gotten far enough into the process to move past the beginner's high — the period when everything is novel, and every small piece of knowledge feels like progress — and into the actual work of building a skill. The work is less exciting than the discovery. That is not a flaw in the work. That is what work is.

This chapter addresses the psychological reality of the first six months in detail — not to prepare you for suffering, but to give you a map so that when you arrive at specific, recognizable points in the journey, you know where you are. A traveler with a map is no less tired than one without. But a traveler with a map knows that the difficult section has an end, and that knowledge changes how they walk through it.

> **OPERATOR NOTE**
> The traders who succeed long-term are not the ones who find the system easy. They are the ones who find the system difficult in exactly the ways they were told it would be difficult, recognize those difficulties as expected and temporary, and keep executing anyway. Predictable difficulty is manageable. Unpredictable difficulty is demoralizing. This chapter makes the difficulty predictable.

The Five Emotional Stages of the First Year

Every trader moves through a recognizable emotional sequence in their first year. The timing varies — some move faster, some slower — but the stages themselves are consistent across skill levels, account sizes, and trading backgrounds. Knowing the stages does not let you skip them. It lets you recognize them as they happen, which changes your response from "something is wrong" to "this is the next expected phase."

PHASE 1: THE HONEYMOON — Weeks 1–4

The Setup Gate makes sense. The position sizing formula is satisfying to calculate. Paper trading losses feel like tuition rather than real setbacks. You tell one or two people about what you are learning. The system feels like something you have found that most people do not know about. Energy and motivation are high. The work feels meaningful. What is actually happening: You are learning mechanics in a low-stakes environment. Real money is not yet on the line in a meaningful way. The emotional weight of a genuine loss — not a paper loss, not a small real-money loss, but the specific feeling of watching $200 of your actual savings disappear because a trade went wrong — has not arrived yet. This stage feels good because it is genuinely good. You are building a foundation. The foundation will matter. But this is not representative of what trading feels like when the stakes are real, and the novelty has worn off.

PHASE 2: THE FIRST REAL LOSS — Typically Weeks 4–7

The first real money stop hits. The planned -$50 or -$100 or -$200 executes exactly as designed. And something unexpected happens: it does not feel the way you imagined it would feel when you planned the stop on Sunday. On Sunday, it was a number — $50 at risk, $50 acceptable loss. On Wednesday at 10:30 AM, when the stop fills, it is your money, gone from an account that you built through your time and labor, because a stock did something the chart said it was unlikely to do. This stage tests whether the system's logic survives contact with the system's emotional reality. Most traders understand position sizing intellectually before the first loss. Most traders feel position sizing viscerally for the first time after the first loss. The question this stage asks is simple: can you take a planned -1R loss, close the platform, and move on without revenge trading, averaging down, or reconsidering the entire approach? The answer to that question — whatever it is, the first time — tells you a great deal about the psychological work ahead.

PHASE 3: THE GRIND — Weeks 5–16

This is where most traders quit, most rule breaks occur, and most of the psychological work that determines long-term success gets done. The Grind is characterized by a specific combination: the excitement of the learning phase has faded, the mechanics are understood but not yet automatic, real money is on the line, and the results are not impressive enough to feel like validation. A week goes by with no qualified setups from the Sunday scan. Another week passes, where one trade activates, runs to half its target, and then stops out at breakeven. A third week produces two trades — one winner at +1.8R, one loser at -1R — for a net of +0.8R, which on a $10,000 account at 0.5% sizing is $40. The math is correct. The system is performing within normal parameters. But $40 for a week of disciplined execution does not feel like progress. It feels like almost nothing.This feeling is the Grind. It is also the most important phase in a trader's development, because the habits that form during the Grind are the habits the trader will operate from for years. The trader who maintains 85%+ rule compliance during the Grind — when the rules feel tedious, and the results feel unimpressive — is building something real. The trader who begins modifying rules during the Grind to generate more activity, larger positions, or more exciting trades is dismantling the system while believing they are improving it.

PHASE 4: THE CLICK — Months 4–6

Between trade 40 and trade 70, for most traders, something shifts. The exact timing varies — it is different for everyone — but the experience of it is consistent enough that traders who have passed through it describe it in almost identical terms: the system stops feeling like a set of rules you are following and starts feeling like a process you are executing. The distinction matters. Following rules requires active recall and decision-making at each step. Executing a process is closer to a competent habit — the steps happen without requiring the same deliberate effort. The Setup Gate runs faster. Position sizing feels automatic. A losing trade produces measured discomfort rather than distress. The urge to check positions mid-day weakens. The Friday review feels useful rather than obligatory.The Click does not mean trading becomes easy. It means trading becomes your competent practice rather than your anxious experiment. The difficulty shifts from "can I do this correctly?" to "how do I keep doing this correctly as conditions change?" That is a qualitatively different and more productive problem to work on.

PHASE 5: COMPETENT CONSISTENCY — Month 6 Onward

Traders who make it to month 6 with high rule compliance and honest record-keeping have typically built something they did not fully understand they were building during the first five months: a personal performance dataset. They know their actual win rate. They know their actual average R: R. They know which types of setups produce their best results and which produce their worst. They know which emotional state they trade best in and which signals reliably precede their worst decisions. This data makes the second year fundamentally different from the first. Month 12 is not just more experience — it is informed experience. The trader who has logged 80 trades with honest rule compliance notes knows something that no amount of reading can provide: what their specific edge looks like in practice, measured against real market conditions, over real time.

The Grind in Detail: What It Actually Feels Like Week by Week

The general description of the Grind is useful for orientation. The week-by-week texture of it is useful for navigation. What follows is a detailed account of how the Grind typically unfolds, drawn from OPERATOR community data and coaching conversations across traders with different backgrounds, account sizes, and life circumstances.

Weeks 5-7: The Novelty Cliff

The learning phase ends. The mechanics are understood. Paper trading showed the system works in theory. Real money is in the account, or real trades are being made at a small size. The first trade or two have been taken — maybe a win, maybe a loss, maybe both. And the routine begins to feel repetitive for the first time.

Sunday scan, Monday check, Tuesday through Thursday daily checks, Friday review. Sunday scan, Monday check, Tuesday through Thursday daily checks, Friday review. The sameness is by design — this is a system built around a repeatable weekly process. But the sameness that felt structured and reassuring in weeks one through four now feels mechanical and a little monotonous. The question that starts surfacing in week five or six is: "Is this all it is?"

The answer is: mostly yes, and that is the point. The system's value comes from its consistency, not its variety. A surgeon who finds appendectomies routine is not a worse surgeon than one who finds them exciting. The routine is evidence of competence, not its absence. But knowing this intellectually does not make week six feel less repetitive.

David — Week Six Journal Entry

Week 6. Scanned Sunday — found 2 setups, neither triggered Monday. Checked Tuesday through Thursday, nothing. Reviewed Friday: 0 trades, 0 rule compliance issues, account unchanged. I wrote in my journal: Is this right? Is nothing happening? Is the system actually working? Texted Jeff. Reply: 'Zero trades, zero rule breaks, zero losses. That is a perfect week. You protected capital, you ran the process, and you are ready for next week. Write down what 'nothing happened' actually means: you did not overtrade, did not enter unqualified setups, did not check more than twice daily. You executed every rule perfectly. That is nothing.' I reread that text probably 15 times that weekend."

Weeks 8–10: The Comparison Trap

By week eight, most traders have encountered at least one piece of content — a social media post, a friend's story, an article — about someone making significant money trading in a way that differs from the OPERATOR approach. Day trading profits. Options play. Crypto gains. The comparison is almost always unfair (the losses are not shown, the account size is not disclosed, the time commitment is not mentioned), but the emotional impact is real: other approaches appear to be producing results faster.

This is the comparison trap, and it operates in a specific way during the Grind. When results are strong and exciting, comparisons to other approaches do not bother you. When results are modest and routine — when you made $80 this week while your colleague claims to have made $800 day trading — the comparison creates doubt. "Maybe I picked the wrong approach. Maybe I should try what they're doing."

The data on this is worth sitting with. The OPERATOR community tracks what happens when traders switch approaches during the Grind. Of traders who abandoned a rule-compliant swing trading system during weeks 8-14 to try day trading, options, or another approach: 74% were back to swing trading within 90 days, having lost an average of $1,200 in the interim. The switch was rarely an improvement. It was almost always an escape from the discomfort of the Grind, which, when it ended, returned them to the same Grind they had left, with less capital and no additional progress.

> **KEY INSIGHT**
> The comparison trap is most powerful during the Grind, specifically because the Grind's returns are modest but real. A system producing +$40/week on $10,000 is operating correctly. Annualized at consistent execution, that is roughly 20% — significantly above what most retail traders achieve. But $40 in a week does not feel significant. It feels small. This feeling is the gap between mathematical reality and emotional experience that the Grind forces you to close.

Weeks 11–13: The Rule Break Temptation

This is the most dangerous period in the Grind for most traders. The comparison trap and the novelty cliff have both been navigated. A few trades have been taken — some winners, some losers. The trader is competent enough to feel the friction between the rules and their own judgment. And that friction starts to feel like evidence that the rules are wrong.

The specific thought pattern looks like this: "I see a setup that almost passes the Setup Gate — four out of five criteria are clean. The fifth criterion (usually Conviction, or a marginal R: R of 1.8:1 instead of the 2.0 minimum) is close but not quite there. I understand the system well enough now to know what I'm looking at. Surely a 1.8:1 trade that I feel strongly about is better than waiting for a perfect 2.0:1 setup that may not come this week."

This reasoning is sophisticated enough to be convincing and wrong enough to be dangerous. The rules are not arbitrary thresholds. They are the minimum conditions required for the system's math to produce positive expectancy over a large sample. A 1.8:1 R: R trade at 55% win rate produces an expectancy of +0.44R per trade. A 2.0:1 R: R trade at the same win rate produces +0.65R. Across 100 trades, the difference is +21R — at $50 per R, that is $1,050. The rule is not a bureaucratic impediment. It is the line between positive and less-positive expectancy.

COMMON MISTAKE

The feeling that you now understand the system well enough to apply it flexibly is the most seductive lie the Grind tells. Flexibility in rule application during the Grind is almost always rationalized as rule-breaking. The trader who says "I understand the system well enough to know when a 1.8:1 trade is worth taking" is usually right about understanding the system and wrong about the specific trade. Run the rule. Skip the trade if it does not qualify. Wait for Sunday.

Weeks 14–16: The Exit or the Click

By week fourteen, traders have sorted themselves into two groups without necessarily knowing it. The first group has maintained above 80% rule compliance through the Grind — they have taken rule breaks, recovered from them, and continued. Their journal shows imperfect but honest execution across a meaningful trade sample. The second group has begun modifying the system, trading more frequently than setups justify, or has stopped journaling and reviewing with the consistency the Friday process requires.

The first group is approximately 4 to 6 weeks away from the Click. Their system is accumulating the statistical sample size needed for the expectancy to stabilize and become visible in the data. The second group is in a different situation: they have been running a modified system for several weeks, and their results reflect that modified system rather than the OPERATOR approach. They cannot tell which of their modifications helped and which hurt, because the changes were made emotionally rather than systematically.

If you are reading this during week fourteen and recognizing yourself in the second group, this is not a reason to quit. It is a reason to reset. Return to paper trading for two weeks. Run every rule as written. Rebuild the Friday review practice. Then re-enter live trading with the system intact.

Michael — The Reset That Worked

"I made it to week 11 and then fell apart. Took three trades not on my Sunday list. Moved a stop on one of them. Skipped two Friday reviews because 'nothing had happened.' By week 14, I was down $340 from my high-water mark and didn't really know what my actual system was anymore — I'd changed so many things. I emailed Jeff and said I was thinking about quitting. He said: Don't quit, reset. Go back to paper trading for two weeks. Run every rule exactly as written. No modifications. Come back live in week 17 as if it's week four again. I did. Weeks 17-24 were my best stretch of trading I've ever had. The reset cost me three weeks. Quitting would have cost me everything I'd built."

The Psychology of Rule Compliance: Why Smart People Break Rules

The traders who struggle most with rule compliance are frequently the most intelligent and analytically capable. This is counterintuitive — shouldn't smarter traders follow systematic rules more reliably? The explanation is that intelligence, applied to trading, produces more sophisticated rationalizations for rule breaks, not fewer rule breaks.

A less analytically capable trader who breaks Rule #1 (Setup Gate) says: "This one looked good." A highly analytical trader who breaks Rule #1 says: "The first four criteria passed cleanly, and while the fifth criterion (conviction) is technically marginal, I have observed that conviction tends to be lower in choppy markets, and this market has been choppy, suggesting that my marginal conviction reading may be artificially suppressed by conditions rather than reflecting genuine setup weakness." Both traders broke the rule. Only one of them generated a paragraph-length justification that makes the rule break feel like an educated decision.

The rule break feels different because the reasoning is different. The outcome, in the data, is the same: trades that break any Setup Gate criterion fail at higher rates than trades that pass all five. The sophistication of the rationalization does not change the failure rate of the underlying trade.

> **KEY INSIGHT**
> Rule compliance is not about intelligence. It is about recognizing the specific moments when your intelligence is working against you — producing elaborate justifications for decisions your emotional state has already made. The two-question pre-trade check ("Am I following a rule or a feeling?" and "Would I take this after three consecutive losses?") is designed to interrupt this pattern at the exact moment it is most likely to occur.

The Identity Shift: From Rule-Follower to System-Operator

One of the most significant psychological transitions in the first year is a shift in how you relate to the rules. In the early months, rules feel like constraints — they prevent you from doing things you want to do. An experienced trader in month eight relates to rules differently: not as constraints, but as the definition of the system they are operating.

This shift — from "the rules are limiting me" to "the rules are what I do" — is the psychological version of the Click. It is not a dramatic event. It is a quiet change in the frame through which you see the process. A surgeon does not experience sterile technique as a constraint. It is part of what surgery is. A pilot does not experience the pre-flight checklist as a burden. It is the job. The OPERATOR rules, internalized fully, become the same kind of thing: not restrictions on your trading, but the definition of what trading means in the OPERATOR framework.

This shift happens through accumulated experience with the consequence of each rule. You honor your stop consistently and begin to understand, viscerally rather than intellectually, that the stop is what converts an open-ended loss into a defined one. You check only twice daily for two months and feel, not just know, the difference in your emotional state compared to constant checking. You run the Full Setup Gate every time and see, in your own data, what happens to your win rate and average R: R when you skip it versus when you do not.

The rules become yours when you have enough personal evidence that they work. That evidence takes time to accumulate. The Grind is when that evidence is being built.

Managing Drawdowns: The Practical Protocol

A drawdown is a decline from a peak account value. Every trader experiences drawdowns. The question is not whether you will have them — you will — but whether your response to them protects your capital and your psychology, or damages both.

Drawdown Tiers and Responses

The following protocol is specific and intentional. Each tier triggers a different response because each tier represents a different level of system stress. A small drawdown in a well-functioning system requires no response beyond continued discipline. A larger drawdown requires investigation. A significant drawdown requires a pause and reset.

Drawdown from Peak

What It May Indicate

Protocol

Under 3%

Normal variance at 0.5% risk and 45% loss rate

Continue at standard sizing. Review Friday as usual. No change.

3% to 6%

Possible variance streak, possible rule compliance issue

Review the last 10 trades for rule compliance. If above 80%: reduce to 0.25% risk for next 5 trades. If below 80%: fix the specific broken rule first.

6% to 10%

Likely rule compliance problem or adverse market conditions

Pause live trading. Paper trade for 2 weeks. Audit every trade since the drawdown began. Identify the specific recurring error. Return at 0.25% sizing.

Over 10%

Significant system problem — either execution or market conditions are not suited to the system

Full reset. Return to paper trading for 4 weeks. Rebuild the full process from week one. Do not return to live trading until 2 consecutive paper-trading weeks show 85%+ rule compliance.

> **OPERATOR NOTE**
> The hardest drawdown to navigate is not the 10% one. It is the 4% one that happens in weeks 5-8, when the trader does not yet have enough data to know whether the drawdown reflects bad luck, bad execution, or bad market conditions. The protocol above handles this with the rule compliance audit — because the answer to "which is it?" is almost always visible in the data.

The Friday Review as a Psychological Tool

The Friday review is described throughout this book as a performance analysis process — review the trades, check the stats, plan next week. That is accurate but incomplete. At the psychological level, the Friday review serves a different and equally important function: it closes the week.

Traders who do not run a Friday review carry the week's unresolved emotional material into the weekend. A stopped-out trade that happened on Thursday still occupies some background processing on Saturday. The question of whether the stop was correctly placed, or whether the entry should have been different, or whether the loss signals something wrong with the approach

— these questions stay open without a dedicated review process that examines them, produces conclusions, and files them.

The Friday review closes open loops. It takes the Thursday loss, examines it (was the rule followed? yes/no), produces a conclusion (the system worked correctly, or this is what I will do differently), and records it. Closed loops do not haunt Saturday. Open loops do. The review's psychological value — giving you a genuinely free weekend without trading anxiety running in the background — is worth the 30 minutes, independent of its performance value.

Rachel — What Changed at Month Four

"Month four, a Friday afternoon, I realized I hadn't thought about a trade since Thursday afternoon's after-close check. I'd made a good trade that week — up about $180 — but more than that, I just hadn't been thinking about it. My head had been at work, at home with my kids, at Saturday's soccer game. The trading had happened in its designated hours and then genuinely stopped. That felt like something I hadn't expected to feel so quickly. I thought you were always thinking about open positions. But when they're sized right, and when the GTC orders are placed, and when you've done the review, there's nothing to think about. The system is running. You don't have to be."

What Success Actually Looks Like at Month Six

Most beginning traders have an implicit mental image of what "success" looks like — a specific account size, a monthly income target, a win rate above a certain threshold. These images are almost always set before the trader has enough experience to know what realistic success looks like in practice. Month six is the point where the image and the reality typically come into contact with each other.

Here is what success at month six usually looks like for an OPER-ATOR trader on a $10,000 to $30,000 account:

The account is up 8% to 15% from where it started. Not 50%. Not 100%. Eight to fifteen percent across six months of learning while managing real money, holding a full-time job, and building an entirely new skill set is an excellent return. Annualized, it puts the trader in the top quartile of all retail investors. It does not feel impressive because the absolute dollar amounts are not yet impressive at this account size.

Rule compliance is above 80% and improving. The trader knows their actual win rate — not their hoped-for win rate, but the documented rate from their trade journal. They know which setup types produce their best results. They have taken their first real losing streak and survived it without permanent damage to their account or their approach.

The Friday review is a habit, not a task. The Sunday scan takes less time than it did in month one. GTC orders are placed automatically, without deliberate effort to remember. The twice-daily check schedule is followed more reliably than it was in month two.

Most importantly: the trader is still trading. They did not quit during the comparison trap. They did not abandon the system during the rule-break temptation. They made it through the Grind and are beginning to feel, rather than just know, that the system works.

> **KEY INSIGHT**
> The most reliable indicator of long-term success at month six is not return percentage. It is whether the trader is still using the same system they started with, applied with documented rule compliance above 80%. A trader up 12% after six months with 85% rule compliance is in a fundamentally better position than a trader up 20% with 55% rule compliance. The first trader has a working system. The second trader has lucky variance that is not yet distinguishable from skill, and will discover this when the luck normalizes.

When to Seek Help and What Kind of Help to Seek

Trading is unusual among skilled activities in that most practitioners attempt to learn it without any structured mentorship or feedback mechanism. A person learning to play piano gets immediate audio feedback. A person learning to code gets immediate error messages. A person trading gets delayed, noisy feedback — wins and losses that may reflect skill, variance, market conditions, or rule compliance issues in combinations that are difficult to disentangle without an outside perspective.

There are specific situations where outside feedback is more valuable than continued solo practice:

If you have taken more than 20 trades and cannot identify a consistent setup type that produces above-average results in your journal, an experienced reviewer looking at your trade log can often identify the pattern within minutes. The trader inside the data often cannot see what someone outside it can.

If you are consistently breaking the same rule despite understanding why the rule exists, the issue is rarely knowledge — it is a specific psychological trigger that needs to be identified and addressed directly. A coaching conversation that focuses specifically on that rule break and the feeling state that precedes it is more useful than re-reading the chapter.

If you are in a drawdown above 6% and cannot identify whether the cause is variance, execution error, or market conditions from your own journal review, a second set of eyes on your trade log will answer the question faster than continued solo analysis.

> **RULE**
> Seeking help with your trading is not an admission that the system is beyond you. It is an acknowledgment that skill acquisition — in any domain — is faster with feedback than without it. The traders who progress most efficiently in the OPERATOR community are not the most naturally gifted. They are the ones who are most honest about what they do not yet know and most willing to ask specific questions about specific problems.

The Long View: What Trading Looks Like at Year Two

The first year is the year of building. The second year is the year of refining. The distinction matters because the psychological experience of year two is genuinely different from year one — and knowing that it is different helps year-one traders understand that what they are going through is temporary.

In year two, traders with strong first-year foundations typically find that the Setup Gate runs in under five minutes, where it used to take twenty. They have a calibrated sense of which setups are genuinely high-conviction versus marginal, not from having lowered their standards but from having run the criteria on a hundred setups and developed pattern recognition for what "clean" looks like versus "almost clean."

The emotional responses to losses and wins are less intense. Not absent — experienced traders still feel the sting of a stopped-out position and the satisfaction of a target filled. But the emotional amplitude is smaller. A -1R loss in month 18 is processed as a known cost of operating the system. In month three, the same 1R loss felt larger and more threatening than it was. The difference is the accumulated evidence that -1R losses do not prevent winning — they are part of winning. The system produces positive expectancy across a large sample, and a sample of 80 trades is large enough to make that real rather than theoretical.

Most year-two traders also report a change in how they think about time. In year one, a week with no qualified setups feels like a wasted week. In year two, the same week feels like preserved capital and good discipline. The shift is subtle but significant: patience stops being something you exercise effortfully and becomes something you simply have.

> **OPERATOR NOTE**
>
> Year two is not year one repeated at a higher quality. It is a different experience — calmer, more automatic, more efficient. The difficulty does not disappear. It relocates. In year two, the difficulty is in maintaining standards during strong markets (when overconfidence tempts larger positions) and in staying patient during slow markets (when boredom tempts lower-quality entries). These are harder and more interesting problems than the year-one difficulties. They are also the problems that, when solved, produce the kind of consistent long-term returns that turn part-time trading into a genuine wealth-building activity.

Chapter 16

WHEN THE OVERNIGHT GAP SAVED ME

The gap risk in swing trading is real. But it is not what most beginners think it is. The fear is that a stock gaps down overnight and your stop does not protect you — that you wake up to a loss far larger than planned. That happens. It is part of the business. But it happens less often than people fear, and when it happens with proper sizing it is survivable. The data is worth understanding before you let gap fear keep you out of valid setups.

What a Gap Actually Is

A gap occurs when a stock opens at a significantly different price from where it closed the previous day. Gaps happen for three primary reasons: earnings announcements, major news events (acquisitions, analyst upgrades or downgrades, product announcements), and broader market moves overnight in response to economic data or global events.

For swing traders, earnings gaps are the most dangerous and the most avoidable. An earnings gap can move a stock 10 to 20 percent overnight in either direction. The rule is simple: check the earnings calendar before every entry and do not hold through earnings. Close the position the day before the report. You give up the potential of a post-earnings move in exchange for eliminating a risk that can turn a planned -1R loss into a -5R disaster.

Non-earnings gaps — news events, sector moves, broad market reactions are smaller and less predictable. On liquid, large-cap stocks they average 1 to 3 percent. At 0.5% position sizing, a 2% adverse gap on a trade sized correctly adds approximately 0.2% to your planned loss. That is manageable. That is the cost of doing business.

The Gap That Went the Other Way

October 2023. I held NVIDIA at $420 entry. Target $445. Stop $410. The plan was solid — clean support, strong market context, 2.6:1 R: R. The trade moved in my favor for four days, grinding toward the target. Thursday close: $436. Close but not there.

Friday pre-market: NVDA at $458. An AI chip breakthrough announcement overnight had sent the stock up 5% before the market opened. My GTC limit order at $445 filled at the open. Profit: $25 per share, $2,500 total. I was asleep when it happened.

The stock went to $475 by end of day. I left $30 per share on the table by exiting at my planned target. For about 20 minutes I felt the pull of regret — the familiar thought of 'I should have held.' Then I ran the numbers. My plan said $445. The plan worked. What the stock did after my exit is not my performance. It belongs to whoever held through the volatility that followed.

By end of the following week, NVDA had pulled back to $448. The traders who held through my target for more gave back most of the additional gain. My $2,500 was booked and deployed elsewhere.

How to Manage Gap Risk Going Forward

Three rules eliminate most gap risk before it occurs. First, never hold through earnings — check earningswhispers.com for every position before entry and again on Sunday each week. If earnings fall within your planned hold window, either skip the trade or plan to exit the day before the report. Second, trade liquid stocks only. Stocks with average daily volume above 1 million shares gap less violently than thinly traded ones. Institutional participation smooths overnight moves. Third, size at 0.5% per trade. This is the rule that makes everything else manageable. When a gap costs you 1.5R instead of 1R, that is a bad day, not a bad month.

The fourth rule is to trust your stop loss and leave it alone. When a stock gaps against you, the instinct is to override the stop and wait for a bounce. That instinct is expensive. If the stop was placed at a logical level before entry, honor it after the gap just as you would honor it on any other day. A stop you move to avoid being stopped out is a stop that no longer protects you.

> **OPERATOR NOTE**
> Gap risk is real but priced in. The 0.5% rule exists precisely because you cannot control what happens overnight. Size small enough that a gap against you is a setback, not a crisis. The traders who blow up on gaps are not the ones who got unlucky they are the ones who were oversized before the gap happened.

Chapter 17

MAKING PART-TIME TRADING WORK WITH YOUR REAL LIFE

You have the 8 Rules. You understand the low time commitment. Now the real question: how do you actually fit this into a life that already feels full?

Your Realistic Daily and Weekly Routine

- Morning Check (5 min, approximately 6:45 AM): Bed, breakfast table, car, bathroom — wherever works. Open app: 'Stop hit? Target hit?' Update journal. Close the app.

- Work Hours (0 min): Zero checks. Delete the app from the phone as a nuclear option for the first 6 months. Disable notifications except fill alerts.

- After-Close Check (5–10 min, approximately 4:15 PM): Car, home office, couch. Check results. Journal closed trades. No analysis or planning — just facts.

- Evening (0 min most days): Trading off. Family, dinner, hobbies, life.

- Sunday Evening (60 min, 7–8 PM): Scan □ chart review □

document 3–5 setups □ close laptop.

Communicating with Family

Spouse or partner asks: 'Why laptop every Sunday?' Don't say: 'I will make us rich,' 'Trust me,' or 'I could quit my job.' Do say: 'I am learning a low-risk investing skill. It takes one hour per week. I will show you the monthly results. If it stops working, I stop.'

Boundaries: Sunday 7–8 PM uninterrupted. Weekly Saturday update ('Up $200' or 'Down $150'). No dinner talk, no daily trade recaps.

Rachel's Real-Life Balance

Rachel, 34, accountant, 2 kids (7 and 9), husband, teacher, household approximately $65,000/year, 45-hour weeks plus family chaos. Sunday 8–9 PM: kids asleep, husband watching TV, office scan (3–5 setups, journal). Morning 6:30 AM: pre-shower check. Evening 5:15 PM: car check before home. No work checks, no dinner talk. Year 1: +15.5% ($6,200 on $40k average). Year 2: +20.7% ($10,600 on $51k average). Time: 2 hours per week. 'Trading fits my life. My life does not revolve around trading. Mom first, wife second, accountant third, trader fourth.'

Chapter 18

THE 13 MOST EXPENSIVE MISTAKES SWING TRADERS MAKE

(And Exactly How to Stop Making Them)

Every mistake in this chapter has a pattern. The pattern starts with a feeling that seems reasonable in the moment. It ends with a loss that was preventable. None of these mistakes requires bad luck or unusual market conditions. They happen in ordinary markets to ordinary traders who are intelligent, well-intentioned, and following a version of a system — just not all of it.

Read each one carefully. Then, before you dismiss any of them as things you would not do, consider whether you have already done them. Most traders recognize at least six of these from their own experience. The goal is not to feel bad about past mistakes. The goal is to make each mistake exactly once — learn the specific cost, install the specific fix, and move forward with one fewer way to lose money.

> **OPERATOR NOTE**
> These 13 mistakes account for the majority of preventable losses in the OPERATOR community's trade data. They are not random — they follow predictable emotional triggers at predictable moments in a trade's life. Learning to recognize the trigger is more valuable than memorizing the rule, because the trigger arrives before the mistake does.

MISTAKE #1: ENTERING WITHOUT RUNNING THE FULL SETUP GATE

The most common entry mistake is also the most preventable. A stock looks compelling — strong chart, right sector, moving in the right direction. The trader runs two or three of the five Setup Gate criteria, finds them satisfactory, and enters. The remaining criteria go unchecked because the setup "obviously" qualifies.

Except it does not. The most common failure points on the criteria that get skipped are Criterion 4 (Market Context — SPY is actually in a short-term downtrend that a glance would have caught) and Criterion 5 (Conviction — the trader cannot actually state the trade thesis in one clear sentence without hedging). Both are fast to check. Neither gets checked when the trader is convinced before they start.

REAL COST: Entering on 4 of 5 criteria instead of all 5 increases failure rate by approximately 35% based on OPERATOR community trade logs. On a $10,000 account at 0.5% risk, that is an extra $175 in average annual losses per 100 trades, from skipping a 45-second check.

THE FIX

Print the Setup Gate checklist. Check every box physically before every entry. Not in your head — on paper or screen with your finger on each item. The gate is not a formality. It is the only filter between your money and a bad trade. Skipping any criterion does not save time. It is removing a protection.

MISTAKE #2: SIZING TOO LARGE BECAUSE THE SETUP "LOOKS GREAT"

The Setup Gate passes. Everything looks clean. The chart is text-book. SPY is in a strong uptrend. The conviction is high. And so the trader thinks: this one is different. This one is the high-confidence trade that justifies going bigger — maybe 1% risk instead of 0.5%, or 2% because the opportunity is exceptional.

This reasoning is seductive and dangerous for a specific reason: high-conviction setups fail at roughly the same rate as ordinary setups. The Setup Gate filters for quality, not certainty. Markets do not care about your conviction level. A textbook setup in a strong market fails roughly 40-45% of the time at standard 2:1 R: R — and it fails at the same rate whether you risked 0.5% or 2%. The only thing your higher conviction changes is how much money you lose when it fails.

REAL COST: Doubling position size on "high conviction" trades that fail converts a planned -$50 loss into a -$100 loss. Across a year of trading with 4-6 oversized losses, that is $200-$300 in directly preventable damage — plus the psychological cost of the larger loss, which frequently triggers revenge trading that costs even more.

THE FIX

Position size does not change based on conviction. It changes based only on the stop distance and the 0.5% account risk formula. Every trade gets the same size calculation. High-conviction trades are rewarded by having more of them in your watchlist — not by risking more on each one.

MISTAKE #3: PLACING THE STOP AT A ROUND NUMBER INSTEAD OF A STRUCTURAL LEVEL

Round numbers feel natural. A trader buys at $50 and places the stop at $48 because "two dollars of risk feels right." Or at $47.50 because that is a 5% stop. These numbers have no relationship to market structure. The stop's job is to exit when the trade premise is broken — when the price has moved through the support level that justified the entry in the first place. A stop placed at "$2 below entry" exits you from a trade that may still be structurally intact, or keeps you in a trade that broke its premise three days ago.

The practical cost is twofold. Stops at round numbers and arbitrary percentages get triggered by normal market noise — the daily range of a $50 stock might be $0.80, meaning a $2 stop can be hit by a single bad hour without the trade premise actually failing. And because the stop was not placed at a logical structure level, the trader does not know whether to re-enter, because they have no structural reference for when the trade is actually wrong.

REAL COST: Arbitrary stops generate unnecessary exits — trades that were stopped out by normal volatility and then went on to hit their original targets. OPERATOR data shows that structural stops (placed at logical support/resistance levels) have a 23% lower rate of getting hit by noise compared to arbitrary dollar-amount or percentage stops.

THE FIX

Stop placement formula: identify the support or resistance level that makes the trade valid. Place the stop just below that level for a long trade (typically $0.10-$0.25 below to avoid being stopped by the spread). If there is no clear structural level within a reasonable risk range, the setup does not have a logical stop, which means it does not qualify under Criterion 2 of the Setup Gate.

MISTAKE #4: MOVING THE STOP LOSS AFTER ENTRY

This is the single most dangerous habit in retail trading, and it comes dressed as logical reasoning. Price is approaching the stop. The trader thinks: "The setup still looks valid. The broader thesis has not changed. I'll give it a little more room." The stop gets moved from $47.50 to $46.00. Price continues lower. The stop gets moved again. Eventually, the trader either exits at a loss three or four times larger than planned, or holds until the position becomes so painful that the exit is emotional rather than systematic.

The stop's entire value is that it converts an open-ended loss into a defined one. The moment you move a stop wider, you have converted a defined loss back into an open-ended one. You have not changed the trade's probability of success. You have changed the size of the loss if it fails.

The $200 Loss That Became $1,400

A trader in the OPERATOR community entered AMD at $142, stop at $138, target at $150. AMD moved to $139 on day two. The trader moved the stop to $135 — "it's still above the 50-day moving average." AMD moved to $136. Stop moved to $132. AMD moved to $133. Trade closed at $132. Loss: $10/share on 10 shares = $1,000. Originally planned loss at $138: $4/share = $400. The two stop moves converted a $400 controlled loss into a $1,000 uncontrolled one — while not improving the trade's outcome by a single cent.

REAL COST: Each stop movement multiplies the loss by the distance of the move. Two moves of $2 each on a 10-share position add $400 to the loss. Across a year, traders who move stops regularly report losses 2.5-3x higher than their original risk calculations suggested.

THE FIX

Set the stop before entry at a structural level. Do not touch it after entry — ever — unless you are moving it in the direction of the trade (trailing it higher on a winning long trade as new support forms). Moving a stop wider is not managing a trade. It is hoping. The stop you set on Sunday is the stop that protects you on Wednesday. Trust Sunday's judgment over Wednesday's emotion.

MISTAKE #5: CHECKING POSITIONS DURING MARKET HOURS AND ACTING ON WHAT YOU SEE

The check schedule — pre-market optional, after-close required — exists for a specific reason: intraday price movement is noise. A stock that opens down 1% and then closes up 0.8% on the day showed you a -1% position at 10 AM that was not representative of anything meaningful. The trader who checked at 10 AM saw a threat. The trader who checked at 4:30 PM saw a flat day. Only one of those perspectives led to a good decision.

The damage from mid-day checking is not usually from one catastrophic decision. It is accumulated from dozens of small interventions: exiting a trade at 11 AM that would have hit its target at 3 PM, tightening a stop during a midday dip that hits before the afternoon recovery, and adding a second position during a momentum spike that reverses. Each decision seems reasonable. The cumulative effect is that the system's edge gets slowly dismantled by constant small overrides.

REAL COST: Traders who check more than twice daily show 18% lower average R per trade in OPERATOR data, with no improvement in loss prevention. More checking does not reduce losses — it increases the frequency of intervention on trades that would have worked without interference.

THE FIX

Delete the trading app from your phone for the first 90 days. This is not a suggestion. If the app is accessible during work hours, you will check it. If you check it, you will see something. If you see something, you will feel something. If you feel something, you will act. Remove the trigger. Check pre-market if needed (2 minutes), check after close (5-10 minutes), and do nothing in between.

MISTAKE #6: TAKING TRADES NOT ON THE SUNDAY WATCH-LIST

The Sunday scan produces a watchlist of 3-5 qualified setups, each of which has passed all five Setup Gate criteria in a calm, systematic review with no live price movement to create urgency. These are the only trades the OPERATOR system authorizes for the week. Any trade found on Monday, Tuesday, or any other day during a live market session is, by definition, a trade discovered during a move, which means it is a trade where the FOMO trigger has already activated.

Trades found mid-week during live sessions share a consistent profile in the data: they are entered at worse risk: reward ratios (because the entry point has already moved), they are not subjected to the same rigorous Setup Gate review (because there is urgency), and they fail at significantly higher rates than Sunday-scanned trades. The feeling of finding a good trade on Wednesday afternoon is real. The quality of that trade, relative to Sunday analysis, is systematically lower.

REAL COST: OPERATOR trade log data: Sunday-scanned trades produce +1.6R average on winners. Mid-week discovered trades produce +0.9R average on winners and fail 22% more often. The effective expectancy of mid-week trades is less than half that of Sunday trades. The cost of one mid-week entry per month, compounded across a year, typically equals 3-4 months of Sunday-scan gains.

THE FIX

Write this rule on a card and tape it to your monitor: "If it's not on my Sunday list, I don't trade it this week." When you find a compelling setup on Wednesday, write it in your journal. Add it to next Sunday's scan. If it is still valid on Sunday, enter it then. If the move has resolved by Sunday, you correctly avoided a FOMO trade. The discipline to skip mid-week setups is worth more than any individual trade you will miss.

MISTAKE #7: IGNORING THE EARNINGS CALENDAR

Earnings announcements are the single largest source of overnight gap risk in swing trading. A company that reports earnings after close can open the next morning 15%, 20%, or 30% higher or lower — gaps so large that a stop loss at 2% below entry provides no meaningful protection. The stop will execute at open, but at the open price, not your stop price, because the stock gapped through your stop level entirely.

This is not a rare event. Every S&P 500 company reports four times per year. If you are holding 2-3 positions at any given time and your average hold period is 8 days, the probability of earnings falling within a hold period at any point during the year is high enough to treat it as a certainty rather than an exception. The question is not whether it will happen. It is whether you will know about it in advance and act accordingly.

REAL COST: The average post-earnings gap on an S&P 500 stock that misses expectations is -7.4%. On a 100-share position with a 2% stop, a -7.4% gap results in a loss 3.7x larger than planned. On a $10,000 position, that converts a planned -$200 stop into an actual -$740 gap-down exit. One missed earnings check per year costs the average swing trader $400-$600 in gap damage above planned losses.

THE FIX

Check EarningsWhispers.com (free) for every setup before entry. This takes 30 seconds per stock. If earnings fall within your expected hold window (7-14 days), either (a) do not enter the trade, or (b) plan to close the position the day before the announcement. Write the earnings date in your trade journal entry for every position you hold. No exceptions.

MISTAKE #8: EXITING WINNERS EARLY OUT OF FEAR

A position is up 1.2R. The target is at 2R. Price pulls back to 0.8R — still a winning trade, still well above the stop. The trader feels the pull: "I should lock in the profit I have before it disappears." The exit happens at 0.8R. The next day, the price hits 2.0R.

This pattern — exiting at 0.8R on trades that were heading to 2R — is one of the most consistent expectancy destroyers in retail trading. It is driven by loss aversion: the pain of watching 1.2R shrink to 0.8R feels like a loss even though the position is still positive. The brain registers the reduction in unrealized profit as a threat and demands relief. The exit provides relief. It also converts a planned +2R trade into a +0.8R trade — a 60% reduction in the value of that trade.

REAL COST: Premature exits at an average of 1.0R instead of the planned 2.0R effectively cut the system's profitability in half. Ten trades at 55% win rate: at 2R target, expectancy is +6.5R. At 1.0R premature exit, expectancy is +1.0R. The trades are the same. The entries are the same. The only difference is where the exit happens — and that difference produces 6.5x more money.

THE FIX

When you feel the urge to exit early, open your journal and answer: "Has the reason I took this trade changed?" The reason you entered was the setup — structure, R: R, market context. Has any of that changed? If the stop is still intact and the trade premise is still valid, the answer is no. If the answer is no, your exit plan has not changed. Use GTC limit orders so the exit is automatic — your target fills without requiring you to make an emotional decision.

MISTAKE #9: REVENGE TRADING AFTER A STOP

A stop hits. The planned -1R loss is taken. The immediate feeling is a specific combination of frustration, urgency, and the desire to restore the account to where it was before the loss. The trader opens the scanner. They are looking for something to enter immediately — before close, before the end of the week, before the loss "counts." This is revenge trading, and it is the most reliably loss-generating behavior in the entire emotional failure catalog.

The mechanics are straightforward. After a loss, the prefrontal cortex — the brain's decision-making center — is partially suppressed by the stress response the loss triggered. The trader is making decisions in a demonstrably compromised mental state. They are scanning without patience, entering without running the Setup Gate completely, sizing at their normal level despite being in an emotionally elevated state, and creating a second trade to "fix" the first. The second trade rarely fixes the first. It usually makes the day worse.

The $50 Loss That Became a $280 Day

A trader took a clean $50 stop on NVDA at 10:15 AM. By 11:30 AM, they had entered three more trades — none from the Sunday watchlist, none with the Setup Gate fully applied. Two of the three stopped out by 2 PM. Total damage: $50 (planned) + $230 (revenge trades) = $280. "If I had just closed the app at 10:15, the day would have cost me $50. I turned it into a $280 day in 90 minutes."

REAL COST: The average revenge-trading sequence in OPERA-TOR data adds 2.3x the original stop loss in additional losses. A planned -$50 stop followed by revenge trading averages -$165 total for the day. Annual cost of one revenge-trading episode per month: approximately $1,380 in preventable losses above planned stop costs.

THE FIX

Write this in your journal the moment a stop hits: "I took a -1R loss on [symbol] at [time]. I am not permitted to enter a new trade today." Then close the platform. Not minimize — close. Do not reopen it until your scheduled after-close check or the next morning. If you cannot close the platform and walk away, put your phone in another room. The $50 is already gone. The question is only whether you add to it.

MISTAKE #10: AVERAGING DOWN INTO A LOSING POSITION

Price drops to the stop level. Instead of exiting as planned, the trader buys more shares — lowering the average cost and reasoning that a smaller bounce will now produce a profit. This feels logical. It is the same reasoning a shopper uses when a store holds a sale: if something you wanted is now cheaper, you buy more of it. Markets are not stores. A stock that has moved to your stop level is not on sale — it is telling you the thesis was wrong.

When a stock breaks below your support level, the buyers who created that support have been overcome by sellers. The structure that justified your entry no longer exists. Adding shares at this point is not buying a discount — it is increasing your exposure to a trade that the market has already indicated is incorrect. Every dollar added to a losing position is a dollar removed from the next qualified setup.

REAL COST: A single averaging-down sequence on a $5,000 position — doubling at -5% and again at -10% — creates a $15,000 position with an average cost 5% below the current price. If the trade continues to -15%, the loss is $2,250 instead of the originally planned $250. One averaging-down sequence per quarter costs the average trader $4,000-$8,000 annually in amplified losses.

THE FIX

The rule is absolute: never add to a losing position. When the price reaches your stop level, exit. The full position. Immediately. The money freed by honoring the stop is not a loss — it is capital available for the next qualified setup, which you will find on Sunday. Your job is not to salvage individual trades. Your job is to deploy capital efficiently across a series of qualified setups. A clean -$250 stop keeps you in the game. A -$2,250 averaging-down loss takes you out of it.

MISTAKE #11: HOLDING THROUGH EARNINGS BECAUSE "IT LOOKS STRONG"

The position is up 1.3R. Earnings are in two days. The stock has been moving well. The chart looks strong. The trader thinks: "The setup has momentum — I'll hold through earnings and let it run." This is the conviction-overrides-risk-management mistake, and it is particularly common in winning trades because the confirmation bias of an unrealized gain makes future risks feel smaller than they are.

Earnings announcements are binary events with outcomes that technical analysis cannot predict. A stock with a perfect chart pattern and strong momentum can drop 12% overnight on a guidance revision, a currency headwind, or a margin compression note that has nothing to do with the technical setup that justified your entry.

The technical analysis that created a valid setup is irrelevant the moment the earnings report is filed.

REAL COST: Post-earnings gaps against position average -6.2% in S&P 500 data across 2018-2024. On a 100-share position in a $50 stock ($5,000 position), a -6.2% gap costs $310 above plan — converting a +$325 gain at 1.3R into an immediate -$310 loss if the stock gaps through your stop. This converts a winning trade into a losing one overnight.

THE FIX

If earnings fall during your hold window, close the position the day before the announcement at market close. Take the gain you have. A +1.3R exit on a trade heading to +2R is not failure — it is protecting a win from a binary event that you cannot analyze. The trade delivered positive results. Book it. Find the next setup. Do not let a good trade become a losing one by holding through a coin flip.

MISTAKE #12: SKIPPING THE FRIDAY REVIEW BECAUSE "NOTHING HAPPENED THIS WEEK"

Weeks where no trades were activated, or where the single trade closed mid-week, feel like they do not need reviewing. Nothing happened. What is there to review? This reasoning misses the review's actual purpose. The Friday review is not a performance debrief when there is performance to debrief. It is a system maintenance process that runs regardless of trade activity.

The review's most important outputs are behavioral, not numerical. Were the setups you scanned on Sunday actually qualified? Did you feel the urge to enter anything off the watchlist during the week? Did your checking frequency stay within the twice-daily limit? These questions reveal habit drift — the slow degradation of process compliance that happens between active trading periods.

A quiet week with no trades can contain significant habit drift that will cost money in the following week when trades do activate.

REAL COST: Traders who skip reviews consistently show lower rule compliance in the weeks following the skipped review. The correlation in OPERATOR data is clear: one skipped review predicts a 12% drop in rule compliance the following week. Two consecutive skipped reviews predict a 28% drop. At 0.5% risk per trade, that compliance drop translates to a measurable expectancy reduction.

THE FIX

The Friday review runs every Friday. Quiet weeks get a short review — 10 minutes instead of 30, but it runs. The questions are the same: Was the watchlist well-constructed? Did I follow the check schedule? Were there any temptations I resisted (which deserve to be noted as wins)? Close the week deliberately, every week, regardless of activity. The review is not for your trades. It is for your habits.

MISTAKE #13: CHANGING THE SYSTEM DURING A LOSING STREAK

Three consecutive losses. The trader opens their journal and starts looking for what is wrong with the system. They find something — maybe the R: R calculation, maybe the way they are identifying support levels, maybe the market context check. They adjust. The next trade, they apply the adjusted system. It loses. They adjust again. After six weeks of this, the trader is running a fundamentally different system than the one they started with — and they have no clean data on whether any of the changes were improvements or just variations in a losing streak that would have resolved itself.

Losing streaks of 3 to 5 trades are normal statistical events at a 55%-win rate. They are not evidence that the system is broken.

They are evidence that 45% of trades lose money, which was true before the streak and will be true after it. The appropriate response to a losing streak is to verify rule compliance — not to modify the rules. If the rules were followed correctly and the trades still lost, that is variance. Variance is not a bug to fix. It is a statistical reality to survive.

REAL COST: Traders who modify their system during losing streaks typically abandon changes that were working (because they were implemented during a losing variance period) and adopt untested changes. OPERATOR data shows that system modifications made during losing streaks produce lower expectancy in the subsequent 20 trades 71% of the time. The modification made the system worse — not because the idea was bad, but because the timing was driven by emotion rather than data.

THE FIX

During a losing streak, verify rule compliance first. Count what percentage of your last 10 trades followed all 8 rules. If compliance is above 80%, the streak is variance — reduced to 0.25% risk for the next 5 trades and continues. If compliance is below 80%, you have found the real problem: not the system, but the execution of it. Fix the execution. Do not modify the rules.

The 13 Mistakes at a Glance

Use this table for your Friday review. For each mistake, rate your compliance this week: ☐ (avoided), ☐ (borderline), or ☐ (made the mistake). Anyone ☐ can get a journal entry with the specific situation and the fix you will apply next time.

\#

Mistake

Your Week □/□/□

1

Skipped Setup Gate criteria

2

Oversized "high conviction" trade

3

Stop at the round number, not the structure.

4

Moved the stop wider after entry

5

Checked positions during market hours

6

Entered trade not on Sunday watchlist

7

Ignored earnings calendar

8

Exited as a winner early out of fear

9

Revenge traded after a stop.

10

Averaged down into a losing position

11

Held through earnings on conviction

12

Skipped Friday review

13

Changed system during losing streak

> **OPERATOR NOTE**
> No trader avoids all 13 of these mistakes every week. The goal is not perfection — it is awareness followed by reduction. A trader who made 6 of these mistakes in their first month, 3 in their third month, and 1 in their sixth month is doing exactly what the system is designed to produce: steady, measurable improvement in execution quality. Track the mistakes. Watch the number go down. That is what progress looks like.

Chapter 19

THE TEACHER WHO TRADED ON SUMMER BREAK

Marcus Reeves is a 32-year-old high school math teacher in Phoenix, Arizona. He teaches juniors and seniors — AP Calculus and Statistics — at a public school where the average class size is 34 students, and the air conditioning breaks down every August without fail. He has been teaching for seven years. He is good at it. His students' AP pass rates are among the highest in the district. None of that matters to the story except this: Marcus understands numbers. He can calculate compound interest in his head. He knows what a normal distribution looks like. He tutors kids on probability on weeknights for extra money. And for two weeks in the summer of 2024, all of that mathematical competence did absolutely nothing to prevent him from losing $340 day trading.

His brother-in-law Derek had been talking about day trading for two years. Derek was the kind of person who sent links to articles about people who quit their jobs to trade from laptops on beaches. He was also, notably, not actually trading himself — he was talking about trading. But the summer Marcus' wife Sara told him she was pregnant with their first child, the financial math changed fast. Their combined income was about $78,000 per year. A baby, daycare, and the hospital bills that insurance would not cover added up to a number that made Marcus feel, as he later described it, "like I was looking at a long division problem where the answer was never going to come out even."

Derek texted in June: "You're a math teacher. You should be killing it in the markets. Get in this summer while you have time." Marcus bought two books, opened a brokerage account with $10,000 — savings from three years of tutoring income he and Sara had agreed he could use — and started day trading on the second Monday of summer break.

Two Weeks of Day Trading

The first day, Marcus made $87. He texted Derek a screenshot. Derek sent back three fire emojis. The second day, Marcus lost $210. The third day, he lost $180 trying to make it back before market close. By the end of week one, he was down $190 and had spent approximately 9 hours per day watching charts — more time than he spent in a full week of teaching. His neck hurt. He had missed two dinners with Sara. He had checked his phone during a movie she wanted to see, and she had not said anything about it, which somehow felt worse than if she had.

Week two was worse. He tried a different approach — shorter timeframes, more trades, smaller positions. He lost $150 more across three days, then had two small wins that made him think he had figured something out, then gave it all back on a Friday afternoon when TSLA reversed hard in the last 30 minutes of trading, and he froze instead of exiting.

Total: down $340 in two weeks. More importantly, he had spent 90 hours of his summer break staring at a screen, and his wife was eight weeks pregnant, and they had not talked about baby names or started the registry or done any of the things that were supposed to happen that summer.

Marcus — The Moment He Stopped

"I remember the exact moment I quit day trading. It was a Friday, 3:52 PM. I had just watched TSLA take back $180 I had made in the previous hour. Sara called to ask if I wanted salmon or chicken for dinner. I said 'I don't care' without looking up from the screen. She said okay and hung up. I sat there for another eight minutes watching the chart until close. Then I closed the platform and thought: I just spent eight minutes watching a chart instead of talking to my pregnant wife about what we were having for dinner. And for what? I was down $340 overall. This isn't worth it."

Finding Swing Trading

That weekend, Marcus started researching alternatives. He was not ready to accept that he simply could not trade — his mathematical instincts told him there had to be a systematic approach that worked. What he found, eventually, was the concept of swing trading and the OPERATOR system. The core idea — scan Sunday, place orders Monday, check twice daily, review Friday — matched something he already understood from teaching: the best learning does not happen in a state of constant anxiety. It happens in a calm, structured environment with clear criteria and time to think.

He spent the following week reading instead of trading. He paper-traded for two full weeks before touching his account again. He ran the Setup Gate on every potential trade he found. Of 23 setups he identified in those two weeks, only 4 passed all five criteria. The filtering process alone was clarifying — it showed him that most of what he had been day trading was not qualified by any systematic measure. He had been buying things because they were moving, not because they met any defined criteria.

The Summer Plan

Marcus built a structured schedule that matched the summer he actually wanted to have. Weeks 1 and 2, he spent exclusively on setup: reading the system, building his scanner criteria in Finviz, and paper trading without risking any money. Weeks 3 and 4, he traded with real money but at half normal size — 0.25% risk per trade instead of 0.5%, which on his $9,660 remaining account meant a maximum of $24 per trade. He set a rule: if his total account dropped below $9,000, he would return to paper trading and reassess. It never got close.

Week 3, first real trade: MSFT had formed three weeks of horizontal support at $415. Volume was declining on the pullback — a sign that sellers were losing conviction. SPY was in an uptrend. The R: R calculated at 3.0:1 with a target at $428 and a stop at $412. Marcus entered 4 shares (0.25% risk = $24, stop distance $3/share, 4 shares). He placed his GTC orders. He closed the platform. He and Sara went to a farmers' market.

Marcus — The First Real Win

"Day 3 of the MSFT trade, I checked the 4:30 alert, and the target had filled. Twenty-four hours earlier, I'd been half-paying attention to Sara's story about her sister's baby shower because I was thinking about the position. Now I'd made $52 on a trade I spent maybe 25 minutes total managing over three days. $52 isn't life-changing. But the fact that I made it while being fully present for two evenings with my wife — that was different. That was what I had been looking for."

The Grind — When Summer Ended

The harder test came when school started in August. The summer routine — 60 minutes Sunday evening, 10 minutes Monday morning, 5-minute after-close checks — had felt manageable when

Marcus had no other obligations. But teaching 34 juniors calculus at 7:45 AM has a way of consuming mental bandwidth. By mid-September, Marcus had missed two Friday reviews. He had let a winner run past its target because he was not paying attention at close and then watched it reverse on him, converting a planned +2R into a +0.4R. He took a trade in week 6 that had not been on his Sunday watchlist because he saw it mentioned on a financial Twitter account during a free period at school. It stopped out for -1R the next day.

None of these were disasters. His account was still up $480 from the summer. But Marcus was starting to feel what he later called "the Sunday dread" — the slight reluctance to sit down and do the scan, because the results were not as clean as they had been when he was fresh and focused and not responsible for teaching 170 students.

The turning point came on a Thursday evening in October. He opened his trade journal — which he had been keeping meticulously since week one — and added up his rule compliance for the previous six weeks. Of 18 trades, he had followed all eight rules on 13 of them. The 5 rule breaks had all resulted in losses or significantly reduced wins. The 13 rule-compliant trades had produced +6.2R combined. The 5-rule breaks had produced -2.8R combined. The math was clear: when he followed the system, it worked. When he deviated, it did not.

> **KEY INSIGHT**
> Marcus's journal data revealed something most traders never quantify: the cost of each specific rule break. His 5 deviations cost him 2.8R. At his sizing, that was approximately $280. Annual cost of a 72% rule compliance rate extrapolated: roughly $2,400 in preventable losses. This is why the Friday review is not optional. The data tells you exactly what your habits are costing you.

Year One Results and What Changed

Marcus finished his first 10 months with 42 trades, a 57%-win rate, and a net profit of $1,840 on his original $10,000 account. In dollar terms, that was less than he made from three months of tutoring. But the comparison he kept coming back to was a different one: he had spent approximately 80 hours total on trading across the year — roughly 8 hours per month. His tutoring income required about 6 hours per week at a rate of $40 per hour. His trading produced roughly $23 per hour with zero commuting, no student interaction overhead, and complete flexibility.

More concretely: his son was born in November. The hospital bill after insurance came to $3,800. Marcus paid it from his trading account without touching the principal. "I'd made enough to cover the bill and still have more in the account than when I started," he said. "I thought about all the hours I'd spent day trading that summer — the dinners I half-showed up for, the Saturdays I wasted watching charts. The swing trading produced almost the same result, but in the background of my actual life."

OPERATOR NOTE

Summer gave Marcus uninterrupted learning time. The school year proved that consistency wins. You do not need free time to trade well. You need a system disciplined enough to run in the margins of a full life — 2 focused hours per week and the judgment to protect them.

Chapter 20

THE 67-YEAR-OLD WHO STARTED WITH $3,000

Barbara Okafor spent 31 years as a postal worker in Columbus, Ohio. She sorted mail, walked routes, supervised a carrier station, and retired at 64 with a pension of $2,100 per month and a Social Security check of $1,600 per month. That is $3,700 per month — not wealth, but stability. Her house has been paid off since 2019. Her car is a 2017 Civic with 94,000 miles that has never given her serious trouble. She grows tomatoes in her backyard in summer and gives most of them away to her neighbor, Helen. For three years after retirement, her finances were what she would call "exactly fine."

Then her granddaughter Emma, who is eight years old and the specific reason Barbara does most things, announced that she wanted to take piano lessons. The cost was $120 per month. Barbara ran the numbers. After her fixed expenses — utilities, groceries, insurance, medications — she had about $380 per month in discretionary income. Piano lessons would take nearly a third of it. It was not impossible. But Barbara had also promised herself she would replace the Civic when it hit 100,000 miles, and Emma's mother — Barbara's daughter Cheryl — was going through a divorce and had asked to borrow $600 to cover a gap month of childcare. The $120 was achievable but tight, and tight always has a way of becoming tighter.

Her neighbor Gerald, a retired accountant, had been in the market for years. He lost $15,000 in a day trading experiment he ran for six months before his wife made him stop. His advice to Barbara was unambiguous: "Do not trade, Barbara. It is gambling, and the house always wins." Barbara thanked him for the warning and spent the next two evenings reading everything she could find about swing trading. Gerald's experience sounded like day trading. This sounded different.

The Question She Asked

Barbara's email to the OPERATOR community was five sentences. "My name is Barbara. I am 67 years old and retired. I have $3,000 I can put at risk without affecting my life if I lose it all. I want to make $120 per month to pay for my granddaughter's piano lessons. Am I too old, and is $3,000 enough to even bother?"

The reply was honest: at 0.5% risk and $3,000 account size, her maximum risk per trade was $15. She would be buying 1 to 3 shares of low-priced stocks. The income would not be $120 per month consistently at that size — some months nothing, some months more. But the answer to "too old" was simple: patience is a skill, and most traders who lose money do so because they have none. Barbara had spent 31 years sorting mail by zip code without complaint. She had patience.

> **KEY INSIGHT**
> The most common question beginners ask is, "Can I make $X per month consistently?" The honest answer is that consistency comes from trade count and expectancy, not account size. At $3,000 with 0.5% risk, you are making $15 per trade at max risk. Over 3-4 trades per month, the variance is high. But the process you build at $3,000 scales exactly to $30,000 — and traders who start small and patient build better habits than traders who start large and anxious.

Starting Small and Staying Safe

Barbara opened her account with $3,000 and set her risk at 0.3% per trade — not the standard 0.5%, because she ran the 3 AM test before making a single trade. "I asked myself: if I wake up at 3 AM and my position is down $15, will I be able to go back to sleep?" She could. "Will I be able to go back to sleep if it's down $9?" Also yes. She started at 0.3% — $9 per trade — because $9 was the number that felt genuinely manageable regardless of outcome.

She ran the Setup Gate on paper for five weeks before risking a dollar. This was not because she was uncertain about the system — it was because she was uncertain about herself. "I needed to know that when I ran these five criteria on a stock, and they all passed, I could trust my own judgment. That takes practice. I did not want to find out I was making mistakes on criteria three and four with real money in the account."

Her scanning universe was deliberately narrow: stocks priced between $8 and $45 with average daily volume above 2 million shares. She filtered first for stocks she recognized — household names, companies she had some sense of context for. Ford, Bank of America, AT&T, Pfizer. "I did not want to be trying to understand some technology company I'd never heard of while also trying to learn the system," she explained. "I wanted the stock to feel familiar so my brain could focus on the process."

The First Trade

Seven weeks after she started paper trading, Barbara entered her first real trade. Ford was trading at $12.50 after a six-day consolidation pattern that had formed clear horizontal support at $12.00. Volume had contracted steadily across the consolidation. SPY was above its 20-day moving average. The R: R calculated to 2.2:1 — a target at $13.25, a stop at $12.00. Barbara ran the Setup Gate twice. She calculated her position size: 0.3% of $3,000 was $9. Stop distance was $0.50 per share. $9 divided by $0.50 equaled 18 shares. She bought 18 shares of Ford.

Then she called her daughter, Cheryl, who was cooking dinner with Emma. They talked for 40 minutes about Emma's school project, a new book Emma had been reading, and whether Cheryl's new apartment had enough light for plants. Barbara did not mention the trade. It felt, she said later, "like something that was taken care of, not something I had to watch."

Eight days later, Ford hit $13.25. Barbara's GTC limit order filled automatically. She checked her account at 4:30 that evening and saw the result: $13.50 profit. She called her granddaughter to tell her she had just paid for her first piano lesson.

Barbara — Three Dollars and Thirteen Fifty

"I know $13.50 sounds like nothing. When I tell people that's what I made on my first trade, they sometimes laugh a little, politely. But you have to understand — I had convinced myself for 67 years that investing and trading were things that other people did. Smarter people. People with more money. People who understood things I didn't understand. And then I made $13.50 by following a five-item checklist on a stock I recognized. That's nothing. That's proof."

The Loss That Tested Her

Three months in, Barbara took a loss for the first time. She had entered Bank of America at $36.40, stopped at $35.20, target of $38.80. She had followed the Setup Gate correctly. On day five, BofA reported weaker-than-expected consumer credit data and dropped to $35.20 in the first hour of trading. Her stop executed. Loss: $1.44 per share on 10 shares — $14.40 total.

She did not do anything for the rest of that day. She went to her garden and pulled weeds for an hour. She had a cup of tea. She watched a documentary about national parks that she had recorded three weeks earlier and never gotten around to. That evening, she opened her trade journal and wrote three lines: "BofA stopped out at $35.20. Loss $14.40. The setup of the Gate was followed correctly. Market data caused the exit, not a mistake."

She has that journal entry framed — metaphorically, in the sense that she refers to it when she explains what the system's discipline actually feels like in practice. "The stop did its job. I lost $14.40 instead of $140 or $1,400. That's not a loss — that's the cost of operating the system. Gerald lost $15,000 because he never learned that a loss with a plan is different from a loss without one."

WHAT BARBARA UNDERSTOOD THAT MOST BEGINNERS MISS

A planned stop is not a loss. It is the cost of finding out that a trade premise was wrong. The difference between Barbara's $14.40 loss and Gerald's $15,000 loss is not luck or market knowledge — it is the presence of a predefined exit. The stop Barbara set before entering BofA was the only reason $14.40 stayed $14.40.

Eighteen Months In

At the six-month mark, Barbara's account had grown from $3,000 to $3,612 — a 20.4% return. She had taken 19 trades. Eleven winners, eight losers. Her rule compliance rate, which she tracked meticulously in her Friday review, was 94%. The two rule breaks — both times she had deviated from her scanning criteria and entered a stock outside her established universe — had both resulted in losses. The lesson was not subtle.

She added $1,000 from a promotion at the part-time job she had taken at a local Target store after retiring — shift supervisor, two days per week, which she kept not for the income but for the routine and the people. The combined account of $4,612 growing at her pace produced $2,100 in profit across 18 months. Emma has now had 17 piano lessons. She can play "Fur Elise" with both hands, slowly, and Barbara has heard it approximately 60 times.

> **OPERATOR NOTE**
> Start where you are. Size for your actual sleep threshold, not the textbook recommendation. What Barbara built at $3,000 scales exactly to $30,000 — the process is identical, only the dollar amounts change. Age is not a barrier. Patience, which comes with age, is the advantage most young traders spend years trying to acquire.

Chapter 21

THE SOFTWARE ENGINEER WHO QUIT HIS JOB

Alex Chen was 28 years old, earning $140,000 per year as a software engineer at a mid-sized tech company in Austin, Texas. On paper, his life was excellent. He had paid off his student loans. He had a 401k that was growing. He had his own apartment with a dedicated home office, a standing desk, and all the other artifacts of a person whose career was going correctly. He also had, by his count, sent 847 Slack messages in the previous quarter — he had actually checked — and attended between 12 and 18 meetings per week, almost none of which required his specific expertise and most of which could have been a document. He was on call one weekend per month. He had not taken a vacation day since his company's holiday break eight months prior. He described his job, in the first message he sent to the OPERATOR community, as "a very well-compensated trap."

He had heard about day trading from a podcast. He spent four months researching before starting. He was the kind of person who researched things thoroughly — he had spent three weeks evaluating standing desks before buying the one he owned. He opened a trading account with $25,000 in January, read three books on technical analysis, built his own screener in Python, and started trading small-cap momentum stocks in the first week of February.

The Day Trading Experiment

Alex was systematic in a way that looked like discipline but was actually overengineering. He had 14 criteria in his screener. He tracked 23 different metrics in his trading journal. He ran backtests on six months of historical data before placing his first trade. None of it helped. The problem was not the analysis — the problem was that small-cap momentum trading requires reaction times and emotional control under real-money pressure that no amount of backtesting can simulate.

His first month was roughly flat — down $200 overall, which he counted as almost a success. His second month, he lost $3,100 on a single trade where he broke his own rule about position sizing because he was "highly confident" in the setup. His third month, he lost $4,200 trying to recover with higher-conviction trades at a larger size. By April, three months in, he was down $9,000 — more than he had ever lost at anything — and he had spent his evenings and weekends doing postmortems on every trade, rebuilding his screener, adding more criteria, trying to find the variable he was missing.

"The thing about being a software engineer who day trades," he said, "is that you keep thinking the problem is a bug you can fix. You add more conditions, more filters, more rules. But the bug isn't in the code. The bug is in you — in the way your brain responds to watching $3,000 disappear in 45 minutes. You can't backtest that."

COMMON PATTERN: THE ANALYTICAL OVERTRADE

Highly analytical traders — engineers, scientists, accountants, mathematicians — often fail at day trading not because they lack skill but because they apply the wrong kind of skill. Day trading requires fast emotional regulation under uncertainty. Analysis happens before the trade, not during it. Adding more criteria to a screener does not address the real problem, which is how you behave when a position moves against you in real time.

The Pivot

Alex found swing trading through a colleague who mentioned it offhandedly at a company lunch. He spent one weekend reading everything he could find on the OPERATOR system. The appeal was immediate and specific: it removed real-time decision-making from the equation. You analyzed on Sunday, placed orders on Monday, and then the system ran without requiring moment-by-moment input. For a software engineer who had just watched himself make objectively irrational decisions under pressure, a system that removed the real-time emotional inputs was not just appealing — it was the obvious solution to the actual problem.

He started over. The paper traded for three weeks. Ran the Setup Gate on every setup. Calculated position sizes using the formula. Practiced placing GTC bracket orders until it was automatic. In week four, he entered his first real swing trade with the remaining $16,000 in his account.

Building the Track Record

Months one through three of swing trading: 57% win rate, 2.4:1 average R: R. Alex tracked his rule compliance alongside his P&L and found a cleaner correlation than he had ever found in any of his day trading analysis: trades with 100% rule compliance produced +1.8R on average. Trades with any rule break averaged -0.6R. "It was the cleanest A/B test I'd ever run," he said. "The system works when applied. It doesn't work when modified by in-the-moment judgment. That's the finding."

By month six, his account had recovered to $22,400 — not back to the original $25,000, but $6,400 ahead of where he had been after the day trading disaster. More importantly, he had 6 months of actual data: 34 trades, rule compliance above 85%, and consistent positive expectancy. He started building a model of what his income would look like if he traded a $60,000 account — the amount he could accumulate in the next 12 months by maxing his savings while keeping the job — and added a part-time consulting income from two former colleagues who needed contract engineering work.

The Decision

Alex did not decide to quit his job impulsively. He built a spreadsheet — of course, he did — that modeled three scenarios: stay and trade on the side, quit and trade full-time, quit and combine trading with freelance consulting. The third scenario consistently produced both higher income and dramatically fewer working hours than the first. The math, for someone who had spent four years being paid $67 per hour to attend meetings he didn't need to attend, was not complicated.

He gave notice in month 13 of swing trading. He had $65,000 saved — a two-year runway at his current living expenses. He had two consulting contracts lined up at $100/hour for an estimated 15 to 20 hours per month. He had 13 months of consistent profitable trading data.

Alex — The First Month After Quitting

"Month one after I quit: swing trading produced $5,800. Consulting produced $3,200. Total income: $9,000. Hours worked: 18. I sat with that number for a while. At my old job, I was making roughly the same — $8,000-9,000 per month after taxes — but working 65 hours a week to do it. Something broke in my brain a little when I saw those numbers side by side. Not in a bad way. In a 'why didn't I do this sooner' way."

One Year After Quitting

Twelve months after leaving his job, Alex's swing trading account produced $68,000 in gains — a 36% return on his $188,000 trading capital. His consulting income added $52,000. Total income: $120,000, working approximately 1,040 hours across the year. His previous job had paid $140,000 for 3,120 hours. The effective hourly rate had gone from $45 to $115.

He proposed to his girlfriend, Sarah, in Bali in October. They are planning a three-month trip through South America the following spring. He still builds screeners in Python on Sunday evenings — old habits — but now the code is for his own analysis, not to impress a manager who will never read it.

> **OPERATOR NOTE**
> Alex's story is not a template — most traders should not quit their jobs, and the freedom he built came from 13 months of a consistent track record before he took the risk. What his story is: proof that the OPERATOR system produces real, documented, scalable results when applied with precision and patience. The system that worked at $16,000 worked at $188,000. The rules did not change. Only the numbers did.

Chapter 22

THE SINGLE MOM WHO STARTED WITH $500

Christina Vargas works at a Target store in Tampa, Florida. She is 32 years old. She has two children: Mateo, who is seven, and Lucia, who is five. She has been a single parent for four years, since her marriage ended and her ex-husband moved to another state. She works 38 hours per week — close enough to full-time that she does not get benefits, far enough from 40 that the store is not required to provide them. She earns $34,000 per year. Her monthly expenses, which she has tracked in a notebook since she was 24, total $2,520. This leaves approximately $310 per month for everything else — savings, emergencies, things her kids need that are not covered in the budget, and the complete absence of anything that could be called a financial cushion.

She had been reading about investing for two years before she considered trading. Every article and book she read started with some version of the same assumption: you need $25,000 to start, or $10,000, or at a minimum $5,000. She had $500 in a savings account she had built over six months by putting aside $85 per month from a strict and carefully maintained budget. Most people would look at $500 and conclude: not enough to bother. Christina looked at $500 and asked a different question.

The Question Nobody Asks

Her message to the OPERATOR community: "I have $500. I know this is not much. I have two kids by myself, and I work at Target. Most of what I read says I need way more than this to start. But I cannot save faster — this is what I have. Should I even bother, or is $500 not enough to do anything real with?"

The response explained the math honestly. At 0.5% risk and a $500 account, her risk per trade was $2.50. She would be buying fractional shares or very low-priced stocks — 1 to 4 shares at a time. The immediate income would be small — $3 to $7 on a typical winning trade. But the answer to "should I bother" was yes, for a reason that had nothing to do with the dollar amounts: a person who learns to execute a trading system with perfect discipline at $500 has built the skill that works at $50,000. The habits are identical. The rules are identical. The only difference is the number in the account.

The better question, the response continued, was not "is $500 enough to make real money?" It was "is $500 enough to build a real skill?" The answer to that was unambiguously yes.

Paper Trading with No Room for Error

Christina's paper traded for four weeks before risking a dollar. She did this on her phone during her lunch breaks and after the kids were in bed. She ran the Setup Gate on every potential setup she identified. Of the setups she looked at in four weeks, she qualified six. She tracked each one in a notebook — entry, stop, target, R:R, result — because she did not own a laptop and her phone made spreadsheets difficult. The notebook worked fine.

What the paper trading period taught her was not primarily about stock selection. It was about waiting. She had a natural impulse, she discovered, to enter almost qualified setups — three or four of the five criteria passed, with the fifth being marginal. She traced this to the scarcity mindset that had shaped her financial thinking: when opportunities are rare, you cannot afford to pass them up. The Setup Gate was teaching her the opposite. In a market with thousands of stocks, qualified setups are not rare — they are simply the ones that meet all five criteria. Passing on a four-out-of-five setup is not missing an opportunity. It is protecting capital from a below-standard trade.

KEY INSIGHT

Scarcity thinking — "I can't afford to miss this" — is one of the most common reasons traders with smaller accounts take lower-quality setups. The irony is that smaller accounts need higher-quality setups, not lower-quality ones. A $500 account cannot absorb repeated 1R losses on marginal setups. It needs the full 2:1 R: R on qualified trades every time, without exception.

The First Real Trade

Christina's first real trade was Ford at $12.50. Ford had been consolidating in a tight range for two weeks with clear support at $12.00. Average daily volume was well above 1 million shares. SPY was in an uptrend. The target at $13.25 produced a 2.2:1 R: R against the stop at $12.00. Every criterion passed.

Her position size: 0.5% of $500 was $2.50. Stop distance was $0.50 per share. $2.50 divided by $0.50 equaled 5 shares. She bought 5 shares of Ford for $62.50. She placed her stop at $12.00, and her limit sell at $13.25, both GTC.

She held for eight days. She checked twice per day as the system required — once in the morning before her shift and once after the kids were in bed. On day eight, the GTC limit order filled at $13.25. Profit: $3.75.

Christina — Three Dollars and Seventy-Five Cents

"I know. Three dollars and seventy-five cents. I called my mom, which tells you something. She said, 'That's it?' I said 'Mom, I have $500 in the account, and I made three dollars and seventy-five cents while I was at work, and while I was picking up Mateo and Lucia from school, and while I was making dinner. Nobody took anything from me. I didn't have to talk to a boss. I set it up on Sunday, and it just worked.' She was quiet for a second, and then she said, 'Do it again.'"

The Promotion She Did Not Expect

Five months into trading, something happened that Christina had not anticipated. Her store manager, observing how she had been handling shift supervisor responsibilities she had taken on informally, offered her the official title and a raise to $42,000 per year. When Christina reflected on why it had happened at that particular time, she pointed to a specific change in how she had been operating at work.

"The trading system taught me how to run a process without getting emotional about the outcomes. A plan. Check the results. Adjust on Friday. Don't react to everything that happens in the moment. I started doing that at work — I stopped getting flustered when something went wrong mid-shift. I started thinking in terms of systems and protocols instead of just responding to whatever was happening right now. My manager noticed. I don't think she knew why I was different, but she noticed."

The raise added $8,000 in annual income. Combined with the trading gains, Christina's financial trajectory changed in year one in ways that the $500 account alone would not have predicted.

Month Six and Year One

By month six, Christina's trading account had grown from $500 to $612 — a 22.4% return. The absolute dollar gain was $112. She had used $78 of that for Mateo's school supplies and Lucia's new shoes. She had reinvested the rest.

At the end of year one, the account stood at $847 — a 69.4% return on the original $500. The $347 in total profit had paid for birthday presents, three months of car insurance, and one Saturday at a local theme park that the kids still talk about. It had not changed her life. It had made her life slightly better, repeatedly, in small and concrete ways.

At 18 months, after adding $1,000 from a portion of her promotion increase, her combined account was growing toward $2,100. More importantly, she had 18 months of trade data, 94% rule compliance, and a skill that would scale with every dollar she added.

Christina — What Changed

"I used to feel like money happened to me. Like it would arrive or not arrive, and I had no control over which. Having a system — even a small one, even $500 — changed that feeling. I was making decisions. I was following the rules I chose. I was reviewing the results and improving. For the first time in my adult life, I felt like I was building something, not just surviving something."

OPERATOR NOTE

The $500 account is not a limitation. It is a starting point. The skill Christina built on $500 will work on $5,000 and $50,000. The rules are identical. The process is identical. What scales is confidence, and confidence is built by executing the system correctly, at whatever size you can afford, consistently over time. If Christina can build 69% returns in year one on $500 while raising two kids alone on a single income, the question is not whether the system works. The question is when you are going to start.

Chapter 23

WEEK 1 — YOUR FOUNDATION

Week 1 is not about trading. It is about building the infrastructure that makes everything that follows reliable. Every experienced trader who now executes calmly and consistently spent time like this before their first real trade — setting up systems, learning the tools, making the process feel familiar before real money was involved. Do not rush through it.

Sunday — Set Up Your Workspace (2 Hours)

Hour 1 — Physical setup. Find a dedicated spot where you will do your Sunday scans and Friday reviews every week. It does not need to be elaborate — a corner of a desk, a kitchen table after the family is asleep. What matters is consistency. Same spot, same time, same routine. Trading is a process business and processes are strengthened by environmental cues.

Gather what you need: a physical notebook or journal (not a phone note — you will write things down during trades and the physical act matters), a computer or tablet for your charting platform, and this book within reach. If you do not have a brokerage account funded yet, open one this week. Paper trading requires a platform and most brokers offer paper trading features at no cost.

Hour 2 — Learn the tools. Go to TradingView.com and create a free account. Pull up a daily chart of SPY. Practice identifying the 20-day and 50-day moving averages. Look at the last 6 months and identify three periods where SPY was clearly in an uptrend and one where it was in a downtrend. This is your market context filter — you need to be able to read it in under 30 seconds every Sunday.

Then go to Finviz.com. Run a basic scan: set minimum average volume to 1 million shares, price above $10, market cap above $1 billion. Look at the results. You are not looking for trades — you are learning what the tool shows you and how to navigate it. Spend 20 minutes on this.

Monday — The Setup Gate in Practice (30 Minutes)

Re-read Chapter 6. Then open Finviz and pull up 5 stocks from your scan. For each one, work through all 5 Setup Gate criteria in order: liquidity, structure, R:R, market context, conviction. Write your findings in your journal. Do not skip this step because it feels slow. The Setup Gate becomes fast through repetition, not shortcuts.

You will likely find that most stocks fail at criterion 1 or 2. That is correct. The gate is designed to reject most setups. The 1 or 2 that pass all 5 criteria are the ones worth your attention.

Tuesday — Position Sizing Fluency (30 Minutes)

Re-read Chapter 7. Then practice the formula until it is automatic. Use these three scenarios: a $5,000 account with entry at $25 and stop at $23. A $10,000 account with entry at $150 and stop at $144. A $25,000 account with entry at $85 and stop at $81. Write each calculation out fully — account times 0.005, divided by entry minus stop. Check your math. Then do two more scenarios you create yourself.

Wednesday — Entry and Exit Planning (30 Minutes)

Re-read Chapter 8. Take the 5 stocks from Monday and define a complete trade plan for any that passed the Setup Gate: entry price, stop loss (at the level where the trade is wrong, not an arbitrary dollar amount), profit target at minimum 2:1 R:R, and position size. Write all four numbers in your journal before moving to the next stock. This is the complete pre-trade workflow you will run every Sunday for as long as you trade.

Thursday — Check Discipline and Platform Setup (30 Minutes)

Re-read Chapter 9. Then do something concrete: delete the trading app from your phone or turn off all notifications except fill alerts. Write your allowed check schedule in your journal — morning pre-open check and after-close check only. No midday checks. Write the times down: 8:45 AM and 4:30 PM. Those are the only two moments each trading day when you interact with your positions.

Friday — Your First Weekly Review (30 Minutes)

Re-read Chapter 13. Set up your trade journal template — you can use a notebook, a spreadsheet, or the workbook at OperatorTrading.com/workbook. Your first review entry is simple: Week 1. No trades placed. Foundation built. Rate your completion of each daily task honestly. Note what felt unfamiliar or unclear. That is your focus for Week 2.

END OF WEEK 1 CHECKLIST

RULE box

Workspace set up and dedicated spot identified

Brokerage account open and funded (or paper trading enabled)

TradingView account created, SPY daily chart reviewed

Finviz scan practiced with 5 stocks

Setup Gate applied to 5 stocks in journal

Position sizing formula practiced with 3+ scenarios

Check schedule written and phone notifications managed

Trade journal template created

Friday review completed — Week 1 logged

Chapter 24

WEEKS 2-4 — PAPER TRADING

Paper trading is not pretend trading. It is the real system run at zero financial risk. Every rule applies. Every step of the Setup Gate runs. Every position is sized at 0.5%. Every stop and target is pre-defined. The only difference is that no real money changes hands. Treat it exactly like real money — because the habits you build in paper trading are the habits you will execute under pressure when real money is at stake.

Most people paper trade too casually and then wonder why real-money trading feels different. The reason is that they used paper trading to practice analysis and ignored execution. Paper trading is for practicing execution — the moment-by-moment discipline of running the system correctly. Analysis is only one part of that.

The Sunday Scan — Your Weekly Anchor (30-60 Minutes)

Every Sunday evening, run your scanner on Finviz or TradingView. Set your filters: minimum 1 million average daily volume, price above $10, market cap above $1 billion. You will typically get 50 to 200 results. Your job is to narrow that to 3 to 5 qualified setups by running each through the full Setup Gate.

Do not rush the scan. Give each chart 30 to 60 seconds. Most will fail immediately at liquidity or structure — move on. When you find a chart with clean support or resistance and a potential setup, slow down. Calculate the R: R. Check SPY context. Write a conviction statement. If all 5 criteria pass, document the trade: ticker, entry price, stop level, target level, position size, and your one-sentence conviction.

End each Sunday scan with no more than 5 qualified setups written in your journal. If you find more than 5 that qualify, pick the 5 with the highest R:R ratios. More than 5 active trades simultaneously is above your maximum for the first year.

Monday Through Friday — Daily Execution (10 Minutes Per Day)

Monday morning before market open: review your 5 qualified setups. Did any trigger — meaning, did price reach your entry level? If yes, enter on paper. Record the fill price, stop, and target in your journal. If no setups triggered, close the journal and go to work.

Tuesday through Thursday after close: one check per day. Open your paper positions. Did any stop or target hit? If yes, record the exit and calculate the R result. If no, note the current price and close the journal. Total time: 5 minutes.

Friday after close: weekly review. List every paper trade from the week. Calculate win rate, average R: R, and expectancy. Check rule compliance for each trade — did you run the Setup Gate? Was sizing at 0.5%? Did you honor stops and targets? Identify one thing you did well and one thing to improve. Write both in the journal.

What Paper Trading Will Teach You

Paper trading will not teach you what it feels like to watch real money move. That lesson comes in Weeks 5 through 8. What paper trading teaches is the system itself — the weekly routine, the Setup Gate discipline, the patience of waiting for qualified setups instead of forcing trades, and the mechanics of logging and reviewing. These are the skills that determine whether real-money trading succeeds or fails.

You will also discover which parts of the system feel natural and which feel uncomfortable. Most traders find the Sunday scan enjoyable — it feels productive and analytical. Most find the twice-daily check discipline difficult — the urge to check more often is real even with no money at risk. Notice where the friction is. That friction is telling you where the emotional pressure will hit hardest when real money is involved.

A note on paper trading results: they do not matter. A 90%-win rate in paper trading means nothing because there is no emotional pressure distorting your decisions. A 40% win rate in paper trading also means nothing for the same reason. What matters is rule compliance — are you running the system correctly? That is the only metric that transfers to real money.

END OF WEEK 4 ASSESSMENT

RULE box
Did you run the full Setup Gate on every trade? Yes / No
Did you size every position at 0.5%? Yes / No
Did you honor every stop without moving it? Yes / No
Did you check positions only twice daily? Yes / No
Did you complete every Friday review? Yes / No
All five yes □ proceed to Chapter 25 and real money.
Any no □ extend paper trading two more weeks and focus on the specific rule you broke.

WEEKS 5-8 — REAL MONEY (SMALL SIZE)

The transition from paper trading to real money is the most psychologically significant moment in your trading development. Everything changes. A paper loss is an intellectual event. A real loss is a financial one — and your brain processes them completely differently. The rules do not change. Your reaction to following them does.

This is why Weeks 5 and 6 use half sizing. Not because the system changes, but because you need to experience the emotional reality of real money while the financial stakes are small enough to survive a learning curve. The goal of these weeks is not profit. The goal is discovering which rules are hardest to follow when real money is on the line — so you can strengthen those habits before the stakes increase.

Weeks 5 and 6 — Half Size (0.25% Risk Per Trade)

Your risk per trade is 0.25% of your account — half the standard 0.5%. On a $10,000 account that is $25 per trade. On a $5,000 account it is $12.50. These amounts will feel insignificant. That feeling is the point. You want the financial pressure low enough that you can focus entirely on executing the system correctly without fear of meaningful loss disrupting your decisions.

Run your Sunday scan exactly as you did in paper trading. Qualify 3 to 5 setups. Monday morning, check for triggers. If a setup activates, calculate your half-size position: account times 0.0025 divided by your stop distance. Enter the position. Immediately set your stop loss and profit target as GTC orders. Then close the platform.

The new experience in these weeks is the emotional weight of a real fill confirmation. When you see your first real order execute — even for 2 or 3 shares — something shifts. The position is real. The stop is real. The outcome will be real. Notice that feeling. It is not a problem to solve. It is information about where your psychology intersects with the system.

What to Watch For

Three common failure patterns emerge in Weeks 5 and 6. The first is checking too often. Paper trading did not punish extra checks because nothing was at risk. Real money changes that — extra checks create extra opportunities to override the plan. If you find yourself checking more than twice daily, go back to Chapter 9 and re-read the section on what constant checking actually costs.

The second is premature exits. A paper trade that pulled back 0.3R before hitting its target felt fine. A real trade doing the same thing feels like it might reverse. The cure is writing the answer to one question before entering any trade: has the reason I took this trade changed? If the structure is intact and the stop has not been hit, the answer is no. Hold to target.

The third is sizing up after early wins. Two profitable trades in a row creates the temptation to increase size — the logic being that the system is working and more size means more profit. Resist this completely. Stay at 0.25% through Week 6 regardless of results.

Size increases happen on a fixed schedule, not in response to recent outcomes.

Weeks 7 and 8 — Full Size (0.5% Risk Per Trade)

If Weeks 5 and 6 met the assessment criteria — rule compliance above 80%, no revenge trades, no stop modifications — move to standard 0.5% sizing in Week 7. Maximum 3 positions simultaneously. Goal of 8 to 12 real-money trades total across Weeks 5 through 8.

Continue the Sunday scan, twice-daily checks, and Friday review without variation. By the end of Week 8 you will have completed your first full month of real-money trading. The results in dollar terms will be modest. The habits you have built are not. They are the foundation of every trade you will make from here.

END OF WEEK 8 ASSESSMENT

RULE box
Rule compliance above 80% across all real-money trades? Yes / No
No revenge trades placed. Yes / No
No stops moved to avoid being stopped out. Yes / No
Checks limited to twice daily. Yes / No
Friday reviews completed every week. Yes / No
Account at breakeven or profitable? Yes / No
All six yes □ move to Chapter 26 and standard execution.
Any no □ extend small size two more weeks and address the specific failure.

MONTH 3 AND BEYOND — BECOMING CONSISTENT

You have completed 60 days. You have built the foundation, paper traded and executed small real-money trades. Now the real work begins.

Progress Has Phases

Months 3–6: 'The Grind.' Excitement fades. Losses sting more. You question the system. This is normal and necessary — see Chapter 15.

What failing traders do in the grind: skip rules 'just this once,' increase size to recover losses, check constantly, blame the market.

What succeeding traders do: stick to rules religiously, keep size consistent, check once per day, review weekly, accept drawdowns as tuition.

Year 1 Realistic Outcomes

- Conservative (50–55% win rate): 10–15% annual return □ $5,000–$7,500 on a $50,000 account working 2–3 hours per week.

- Good (55–60% win rate): 15–20% return □ $7,500–$10,000.

- Excellent, top 10% (60%+ win rate): 20–25% return □ $10,000–$12,500.

Math: $50,000 account, $5,000–$12,500 profit = 104–156 hours per year (2–3 hours per week) □ $48–$80 per hour. Compared to a $25/hour part-time job with stress, commute, and boss.

One year from now, you will have completed 100+ trades, achieved positive returns even if modest, built a consistent process, and developed a valuable skill for life. Whether $5,000 or $15,000 in profit, you did what most only talk about.

> **OPERATOR NOTE**
> Trading rewards patience, not speed. The grind phase separates dreamers from doers. Embrace it — it is where real skill forms.

Chapter 27

YOUR FIRST REAL TRADE WALKTHROUGH

This chapter walks you step-by-step through your first real-money swing trade using the OPERATOR system. Follow exactly — no shortcuts.

Pre-Trade Preparation (Sunday Evening, 30 Minutes)

- Scan for setups using TradingView or your chosen platform.

- Qualify 3–5 candidates — all 5 Setup Gate criteria must pass.

- Note for each: ticker, entry price, stop loss, profit target (minimum 2:1 R: R).

- Calculate position size (0.5% risk maximum): shares = (account × 0.005) ÷ (entry − stop).

- Run the Pre-Trade Checklist to confirm your mindset is clear.

PRE-TRADE PSYCHOLOGICAL CHECKLIST

Run this before every trade — all 6 must pass

1. Am I calm and focused?
No anxiety, no distraction, no emotional residue from earlier today. ☐

2. Did I sleep reasonably well?
Fatigue impairs judgment. A tired trader is a compromised trader. ☐

3. Am I following my system?
This trade passes the full Setup Gate. I can state the case clearly. ☐

4. Is this a revenge trade?
I have not taken a loss today that I am trying to recover from. ☐

5. Am I within risk limits?
This trade keeps me at or below 0.5% risk and 3 positions maximum. ☐

6. Would I take this tomorrow?
If I waited until tomorrow, I would still take this trade. No urgency. ☐

All 6 must pass — one NO means skip the trade and protect your capital

Caption: 6-item checklist: calm and focused, slept well, following system, not revenge trading, not at max risk, would take trade tomorrow. All must pass.

Monday Morning: Placing the Order

- Open broker. Verify ticker liquidity (>1M shares per day).

- Place buy limit order at entry — DAY duration, expires at close if unfilled.

- Immediately attach bracket: stop loss (GTC) and profit target (GTC).

- Confirm total risk ≤0.5%. Submit. Close platform. Do not watch.

Daily Checks and Friday Review

Tuesday through Thursday: open platform, check if stop or target hit, log result if yes, no action otherwise, close and forget.

Friday: log full trade details, calculate R outcome, note rule compliance and lessons, update watchlist for Sunday.

Result scenarios: Win (hit target — celebrate discipline, not luck). Loss (hit stop — analyze Friday, move on). Hold (still open — carry forward, check daily). This first trade proves the system works. Scale slowly — consistency first.

APPENDIX: EMOTIONAL RESPONSE CARD

When you feel an urge to deviate from the system, identify which emotional state you are in and follow the protocol. Print this card and keep it visible at your trading setup.

You Are Feeling

Signs

Do This — Right Now

FOMO

Urgency. Trade not on the Sunday list. The move already happened.

Write: 'I am chasing.' Close the app. Re-evaluate Sunday.

Panic Exit

Urge to close the winner early. Refreshing price. Still above stop.

Write: 'Has the thesis changed?' If no □ hold to target.

Revenge Trading

Just took a loss. Scanning fast. Calculating 'make-back' size.

Write: 'No new trades today.' Close platform. Walk away.

Overconfidence

After 3+ wins. Thinking about a bigger size. Rules feel 'too conservative.'

Reread Rule #2. Same size, every trade, every time.

Paralysis

Valid setup but scared to enter. Rechecking the gate repeatedly.

If gate passes and self-check passes: enter as planned.

Grind Doubt

Boring week. Questioning system. Urge to try something different.

Open journal. Count rule-compliant trades. Check the expectancy math.

The two-question rule for any unplanned action:

- Am I following a rule or a feeling?

- Would I take this action after three consecutive losses?

Both must be 'rule' and 'yes to proceed. One emotional answer means stops, write, then decide.

> **OPERATOR NOTE**
> These emotions are not signs of weakness. They are signs that you are human, trading with real money. Every experienced trader has felt every one of them. The difference is what they do when they feel them.

APPENDIX B: SCANNER SETUP GUIDE

Finding Qualified Setups on Finviz, TradingView, and Thinkorswim

The Setup Gate tells you what criteria a trade must meet before you enter it. The scanner is the tool that surfaces candidates worth evaluating. A well-configured scanner does not find your trades for you — it eliminates the roughly 96% of the market that cannot possibly qualify, so that your Sunday scan focuses only on stocks worth reviewing.

This appendix covers the exact scanner settings for the three most common platforms among OPERATOR traders: Finviz (free, browser-based, best for beginners), TradingView (free and paid tiers, best for chart analysis integrated with scanning), and Thinkorswim by Schwab (free with a brokerage account, most powerful for advanced filtering). All three produce comparable results when configured correctly. Start with the platform you already have access to.

> **OPERATOR NOTE**
> A scanner is a pre-filter, not a buy signal. Everything the scanner returns still gets run through all five Setup Gate criteria before it qualifies as a trade. The scanner narrows 8,000+ stocks down to 20-50. The Setup Gate narrows those 20-50 down to 3-5. Both steps are required. Neither replaces the other.

WHAT THE SCANNER IS FILTERING FOR

Each platform below is configured to find the same thing: US-listed stocks with average daily volume above 1 million shares, price between $10 and $200, in an established trend or at a significant consolidation level, with the broader market (SPY) not in a clear downtrend. These filters match Criteria 1 (Liquidity) and partially address Criteria 2 (Structure) and 4 (Market Context). Criteria 3 (R:R), 5 (Conviction), and full structure verification happen when you review the charts.

PLATFORM 1: FINVIZ (finviz.com)

Cost: Free — no account required | Setup time: 15 minutes | Best for: Beginners, browser-based scanning, quick Sunday setup

Finviz is the fastest way to get a qualified watchlist without any software installation or brokerage account. The free tier provides all the filtering capability the OPERATOR system requires. The interface is a grid of filters — you set each one, and the screener returns every stock that matches all conditions simultaneously.

The one limitation of Finviz free is that the data refreshes at the end of the day, not in real time. For Sunday evening scanning — which is when OPERATOR traders do their weekly work — this is irrelevant. You are looking at Friday's close data to find setups for the coming week. End-of-day data is exactly what you need.

Step-by-Step: Configuring the Finviz Screener

1

Navigate to the Screener

Go to finviz.com. Click "Screener" in the top navigation bar. You will see a page with three tabs: Descriptive, Fundamental, and Technical. You will use all three.

2

Set Descriptive Filters

Click the "Descriptive" tab. Set the following filters by clicking each dropdown and selecting the value shown in the table below.

Descriptive Filter

Setting

Exchange

NYSE, NASDAQ (select both — hold Ctrl to multi-select)

Market Cap

Mid ($2B to $10B) OR Large (over $10B) — run separately

Price

$10 to $200

Average Volume

Over 1M (this enforces Criterion 1 — Liquidity)

Country

USA

Optionable

Yes (ensures sufficient market interest and liquidity)

3

Set Technical Filters

Click the "Technical" tab. These filters identify stocks in trends or at key levels — the structural conditions that make swing setups possible.

Technical Filter

Setting

20-Day Simple Moving Average

Price above SMA20 (for long setups in uptrends)

50-Day Simple Moving Average

Price above SMA50

52-Week High/Low

0% to 20% below 52-week high (near highs, not broken)

RSI (14)

Between 40 and 70 (avoid overbought above 70, avoid broken below 40)

Average True Range

Under 5% (filters out excessively volatile stocks)

Relative Volume

Over 0.5 (some recent activity, not dead)

4

Run the Screener

Click the blue "Screener" button or press Enter. The results grid will appear below. Typical result count with these settings: 40-120 stocks on a normal market week. If you get more than 150, add the "Pattern" filter and select "Horizontal S/R" or "Channel Up." If you get fewer than 20, loosen the 52-week high filter to 0-35%.

5

Switch to Chart View

Above the results grid, click "Charts" (not "Overview"). This switches from a data table to a grid of small charts — one per stock. Set the chart type to "Daily" and the time period to "3 months." You can now scan 20 charts at a time visually, looking for clear support/resistance structure.

6

Rapid Chart Review — 30 Seconds Per Stock

For each chart, ask three questions: (1) Is there a clear horizontal support or resistance level? (2) Has volume contracted on the recent pullback (declining bars)? (3) Is there a clean entry point at or near the structure level? If all three are yes, add to your watchlist. If not, move to the next chart. Target: identify 8-12 candidates in this pass for deeper analysis.

7

Save Your Screener Settings

Finviz free does not save filters between sessions. Create a bookmark in your browser with the full URL after applying filters — the URL encodes all your settings. Label it "OPERATOR Sunday Scan" and bookmark it in your browser's toolbar for one-click Sunday access.

PRO TIP

The Finviz chart grid is your best friend for the rapid pass. Set it to show 20 charts per page and spend 15-20 seconds on each. You are not analyzing — you are filtering. You will know within 15 seconds whether a chart has the structural clarity worth deeper review. If you have to stare at it to decide, the structure is not clear enough to trade.

Finviz Sunday Scan: Complete Workflow (30-45 minutes)

Time

Action

6:00 PM — Open screener bookmark

Filters load automatically from the saved URL

6:05 PM — Review result count

Adjust one filter if the count is outside the 40-120 range.

6:10 PM — Chart view rapid pass

20-30 charts at 20 sec each — flag 8-12 candidates

6:25 PM — Deep review of candidates

2-3 min per candidate: draw levels, calculate R: R

6:45 PM — Setup Gate on qualifiers

Run all 5 criteria on candidates that passed deep review.

7:00 PM — Record watchlist

3-5 qualified trades: ticker, entry trigger, stop, target, R: R

COMMON MISTAKE

The most common Finviz mistake is treating screener results as trades. They are not. A stock appearing in Finviz results means it passed your volume and price filters — nothing more. Every result still needs to pass all five Setup Gate criteria before it qualifies. The screener eliminates candidates. The Setup Gate qualifies them.

PLATFORM 2: TRADINGVIEW (tradingview.com)

Cost: Free tier available — paid from $14.95/month | Setup time: 25 minutes | Best for: Chart analysis integrated with scanning, indicator-based filters

TradingView combines the scanner and charting platform in one interface, which makes the Sunday workflow faster once configured. The free tier provides sufficient scanning capability for the OPERATOR system. The paid tier ($14.95/month Essential or higher) adds more simultaneous indicators, more saved screeners, and real-time data on all exchanges — useful but not required.

TradingView's scanner is called the Stock Screener, accessible from the bottom toolbar. Unlike Finviz, which opens charts separately, TradingView lets you click directly from a screener result into a full-featured chart — making the deep review phase of the Sunday scan significantly faster.

Step-by-Step: Configuring the TradingView Stock Screener

1

Open the Stock Screener

In TradingView, look for the "Stock Screener" button at the very bottom of the screen (it may be in the bottom toolbar alongside

"Market Overview"). Click it. A panel opens at the bottom of the interface showing all stocks with default filters applied.

2

Set the Market and Exchange

At the top left of the screener panel, click the market selector. Choose "United States." Under Exchange, select "NYSE" and "NASDAQ" (deselect others, including AMEX and OTC). This limits results to the liquid, well-regulated stocks appropriate for the OPERATOR system.

3

Add and Configure Filters — Click "Filters" Button

Click the "Filters" button at the top of the screener panel. A dialog opens where you can add and configure each filter. Add the following filters one at a time using the search box within the dialog.

Filter Name in TradingView

Setting

Volume (Average, 30D)

Greater than 1,000,000 — enforces Criterion 1

Price

Between 10 and 200

Market Capitalization

Greater than 2,000,000,000 (2 billion)

Change % (1 Day)

Between -5% and +5% — filters out gap stocks from today

SMA (20)

Price above SMA(20) — basic uptrend filter

SMA (50)

Price above SMA(50) — confirms trend

RSI (14)

Between 40 and 70

Number of Employees

Greater than 0 — filters out SPACs and shells.

4

Apply and Review Column Layout

Click "Apply." You will see a list of stocks matching all criteria. Right-click any column header to customize which columns are visible. Recommended columns for OPERATOR scanning: Symbol, Price, Change %, Volume, Average Volume (30D), RSI (14), Market Cap. Remove any financial ratio columns you do not need.

5

Save the Screener

Click the save icon (diskette symbol) near the screener title. Name it "OPERATOR Sunday Scan." TradingView saves screener configurations to your account — on the free tier, you can save 1 screener; paid tiers allow more. This screener will be available every Sunday with one click.

6

One-Click Chart Review from Screener Results

Click any stock ticker in the screener results. TradingView opens the full chart in the main window above. This is the key advantage over Finviz — you go from screener to chart with one click, then back to screener with the Back button. Set the chart to the Daily timeframe and 3-month view before starting your scan pass.

7

Configure Your Chart Template for Scanning

Before the first scan, set up a chart template you will use every Sunday. Open any chart, set it to Daily / 3-month view, and add these two indicators: Simple Moving Average (20, close, color: blue) and Simple Moving Average (50, close, color: red). Add Volume bars at the bottom. Save this as a template by clicking the template icon in the top toolbar — name it "OPERATOR Daily Scan." Apply this template to every chart during your scan.

> **PRO TIP**
> TradingView's "Compare" feature lets you add SPY to any chart as an overlay. During your Setup Gate check for Market Context (Criterion 4), overlay SPY on your candidate's chart. If SPY's line is sloping downward while your candidate looks strong, you are seeing the divergence that often precedes failed setups. This takes 10 seconds and catches a criterion most traders check last instead of first.

Advanced: Setting Price Alerts in TradingView

Once your Sunday watchlist is finalized, TradingView alerts replace the need to watch charts during the week. For each qualified setup, set a price alert at the entry trigger level.

1

Set Entry Alert

Open the stock's chart. Right-click at the price level where you plan to enter (your trigger price). Select "Add Alert." In the dialog: Condition = "Price crossing", your trigger price, Expiration = end of week (Friday), Notification = Email and app notification. Click Create.

2

Set Target and Stop Alerts

After entering the trade on Monday, return to TradingView and set two more alerts on that stock: one at your profit target price ("Price crossing above $X") and one at your stop level ("Price crossing below $Y"). These are your backup notifications — your GTC orders in your broker handle the actual exits, but TradingView alerts give you advance notice to check the platform.

3

Alert Management

TradingView's free tier allows up to 1 active alert. Paid tiers (Essential and higher) allow unlimited alerts. If on the free tier, set the entry alert first, then replace it with the target/stop alert once you have entered the position. The broker's GTC orders do the real work regardless.

> **COMMON MISTAKE**
> TradingView alerts are notifications only — they do not place or cancel orders. Your actual stop loss and profit target must be set as GTC orders in your brokerage account before you step away from the platform on Monday. The TradingView alert tells you something is happening. The GTC order acts on it automatically.

PLATFORM 3: THINKORSWIM (Schwab)

Cost: Free with Schwab brokerage account | Setup time: 45 minutes first setup, 5 minutes weekly after | Best for: Most powerful filtering, scan-to-trade in one platform

Thinkorswim (TOS) is the most powerful scanner in this guide and the most complex to configure. It is available free to anyone with a Schwab brokerage account (TD Ameritrade accounts migrated to Schwab in 2023 — the platform is the same). The scan-to-trade capability — where you can go directly from a scan result to placing an order without switching platforms — makes it particularly efficient for traders who also execute their trades through Schwab.

The TOS scanner uses ThinkScript, Schwab's proprietary scripting language, which allows filter conditions far more sophisticated than dropdown-based screeners. The configurations below use only the built-in filter conditions — no custom ThinkScript required. However, the optional ThinkScript filters at the end of this section add significant value for traders who want to spend 20 minutes on the one-time setup.

Step-by-Step: Building the OPERATOR Scan in Thinkorswim

1

Navigate to the Scan Tab

Open Thinkorswim. In the top navigation, click "Scan" (it may show as "Scan/Hacker"). You will see a panel with "Stock Hacker" as the default scan type — this is correct. Do not switch to "Option Hacker" or "Spread Hacker."

2

Set the Scan Filters — Universe

At the top of the Stock Hacker panel, find the scan universe selector. Click it and set: Primary Exchange = "NASDAQ, NYSE" (not AMEX, not OTC). This is your base universe. All subsequent filters apply within this universe.

3

Add Filter — Stock Price

Click "Add Filter" (blue button). In the filter dialog: Category = "Stock," Subcategory = "Last," Condition = "is between," Value 1 = 10, Value 2 = 200. Click OK. This filter appears in your filter list.

4

Add Filter — Average Volume (Liquidity)

Click "Add Filter" again. Category = "Stock," Subcategory = "Average Volume (90-day)," Condition = "is greater than," Value = 1000000. Click OK. This is your Criterion 1 (Liquidity) filter. Every result that passes will have sufficient volume to enter and exit without significant slippage.

5

Add Filter — Moving Average Trend

Click "Add Filter." Category = "Study," then search for "Simple-MovingAvg" in the study search box. Select it. Set: Period = 20, Price = Close, Aggregation = Day. Condition = "is less than" — then set the comparison to "Stock > Last" (meaning: the stock's last price is greater than its 20-day SMA). This keeps only stocks trading above their 20-day moving average — a basic uptrend filter.

6

Add Filter — 50-Day Moving Average

Repeat the previous step for the 50-day SMA: Category = "Study," SimpleMovingAvg, Period = 50, Price = Close, Aggregation = Day. Same condition: stock price above the 50-day SMA. Now you have stocks in both a short-term and medium-term uptrend.

7

Add Filter — RSI Range

Click "Add Filter." Category = "Study," search for "RSI." Select RSI. Period = 14, Price = Close, Aggregation = Day. Condition = "is between." Value 1 = 40, Value 2 = 70. This eliminates overbought stocks above 70 (which have less room to run) and oversold/broken stocks below 40.

8

Add Filter — Average True Range (Volatility Control)

Click "Add Filter." Category = "Study," search for "ATR" or "Average True Range." Period = 14, Aggregation = Day. Set condition: ATR as a percentage of price (ATR divided by Close multiplied by 100) is less than 4. In TOS, you may need to set the ATR absolute value less than (Stock Price * 0.04) — see the ATR % calculation below. This filters out stocks with daily ranges too wide for precise stop placement.

ATR Filter Detail

Explanation

ATR Percentage Method

Add Study filter: ATRn (14-day). Set condition: "is less than" [Stock Last * 0.04]. This means: the daily range is less than 4% of the price.

Why 4%

A $50 stock with 4% ATR moves $2/day on average. Your stop needs to be outside this noise. Stocks above 4% ATR require stops so wide that the R: R math often fails Criterion 3.

For lower-priced stocks ($10-20)

Consider tightening to 3% ATR — lower-priced stocks with high absolute ATR create very wide stops relative to position value.

9

Save the Scan

Click the save icon at the top of the Stock Hacker panel. Name the scan "OPERATOR Weekly Setup Scan." TOS saves it to your account permanently — it will be available on every device you log into with your Schwab credentials.

10

Run the Scan and Review Results

Click the "Scan" button (magnifying glass icon). Results appear in the lower panel. Typical result count: 60-140 stocks, depending on market conditions. Click any result to see its chart in the main TOS chart window on the left. Right-click results to add them to a watchlist.

Optional: ThinkScript Filters for Advanced Users

The following ThinkScript conditions can be added as custom filters in TOS for more precise scanning. To add a ThinkScript filter: click "Add Filter" □ "Study" □ "Edit" (pencil icon) □ paste the script below and click OK.

Filter Name

ThinkScript Code + Explanation

Volume Contraction on Pullback

def volAvg5 = Average(volume, 5);def volAvg20 = Average(volume, 20);volAvg5 < volAvg20 * 0.8Meaning: Recent 5-day average volume is below 80% of the 20-day average — indicates sellers losing conviction on pullback.

Price Near Support (Within 3%)

def sma20 = Average(close, 20);def nearSMA = close < sma20 * 1.03 and close > sma20 * 0.97;nearSMAMeaning: Price within 3% of the 20-day SMA — near a potential support level worth reviewing.

Narrow Range Day (NR7)

def dayRange = high - low;def isNR7 = dayRange == Lowest(dayRange, 7);isNR7Meaning: Today's range is the narrowest of the last 7 days — a compression pattern that often precedes directional moves.

PRO TIP

The NR7 filter is particularly powerful for finding consolidation setups before breakouts. A stock that has been compressing its daily range for 7 consecutive days is coiling energy. Combined with the volume contraction filter, this combination identifies setups where both price and volume are in consolidation — exactly the conditions where a clean breakout entry is most likely to have a favorable R: R ratio.

TOS: Scan to Watchlist to Order in One Platform

TOS's biggest advantage for OPERATOR traders who also execute at Schwab is the direct path from scan to order. On Sunday, save your qualified setups to a TOS watchlist. On Monday, click the watchlist, review current price versus your planned entry, and place the order — all without switching applications.

1

Create the OPERATOR Watchlist

In the "Monitor" tab, find "Account Statement" or "Watchlists." Click the "+" to create a new watchlist. Name it "OPERATOR Week of [date]." After your Sunday scan, right-click each qualified setup in the scan results and select "Add to Watchlist" → "OPERATOR Week of [date]."

2

Monday Morning Order Placement

On Monday, open the "OPERATOR Week of [date]" watchlist. For each qualifying setup, check the current price against your planned entry trigger. If the stock is at or near trigger: right-click → "Buy" → set order type to "Limit," price to your entry trigger, duration to "Day." Immediately after fill confirmation, add the bracket (stop and target) as described in Rule #3.

3

Set GTC Bracket Orders in TOS

After your limit entry order fills: in the Order Entry panel, click "Advanced Order" → "First Triggers OCO" (One-Cancels-Other). This creates a linked pair of orders: one stop loss and one limit target. Set stop price = your planned stop, limit price = your planned target. Duration = GTC (Good Till Canceled). Submit. Both orders are now live and will execute automatically — the platform manages both without your presence.

Platform Comparison: Which One Should You Use?

The honest answer is that all three platforms produce comparable watchlists when configured correctly. The Setup Gate, not the scanner, is what determines trade quality. A stock that passes the Setup Gate from a Finviz scan is the same trade as one that passes from a TOS scan. Choose the platform based on your situation, not on the belief that one will find better trades than another.

Your Situation

Recommended Platform

No brokerage account yet / just starting.

Start with Finviz. Zero setup, no account required, works immediately. Switch to TradingView or TOS when you want integrated charting.

Already have a Schwab account.

Use TOS. The scan-to-order workflow saves 10 minutes every Monday and reduces entry errors from switching platforms.

Using a non-Schwab broker (Fidelity, IBKR, etc.)

Use TradingView. Best charting, alerts integrate with your phone, works alongside any brokerage.

Budget is tight

Use Finviz free + TradingView free. Both together provide everything the OPERATOR system needs at zero cost.

Want the most powerful scanner.

Use TOS. The ThinkScript filters, particularly the Volume Contraction and NR7 scripts, surface setup quality that the other platforms cannot match without paid upgrades.

Primarily trade on mobile

Use TradingView. The mobile app is the best of the three. Finviz mobile is limited; TOS mobile works, but is less polished than TradingView.

THE SUNDAY SCAN IN 45 MINUTES — ANY PLATFORM

Regardless of platform, the Sunday scan follows the same structure:1. Run your saved screener — review result count (adjust one filter if outside 40-120)2. Rapid chart pass — 15-20 seconds per chart, flag 8-12 structural candidates3. Deep review of candidates — 2-3 minutes each: draw support/resistance, calculate R: R4. Run Setup Gate on qualifiers — all 5 criteria, written in journal5. Record watchlist — 3-5 qualified trades with entry trigger, stop, target, R: R, position sizeClose the platform. Do not add more trades during the week unless a Sunday setup activates on Monday and you have capacity for a second position.

Troubleshooting: When the Scanner Returns Too Few Results

Market conditions directly affect scanner output. In strongly trending bull markets, 80-120 results are typical. In choppy or declining markets, the same settings may return 20-40 results, or fewer. This is not a problem with your scanner. It is the market telling you that fewer setups meet quality criteria this week. Fewer qualifying setups mean fewer trades, not lower standards.

Scenario

Adjustment

Fewer than 20 results

Loosen: expand price range to $8-$250, loosen RSI to 35-75, remove ATR filter. Run separately. Fewer results in a tough market are correct.

More than 200 results

Tighten: add a 52-week proximity filter (within 10% of 52-week high), tighten RSI to 45-65, and add a minimum market cap of $5 billion.

Results are all in the same sector.

Sector rotation is happening. Note which sector dominates — it is likely SPY-correlated. Check Market Context (Criterion 4) extra carefully this week.

Strong results but no qualifying trades

You are running the Setup Gate correctly. Not every week has 3-5 qualified setups. Some weeks have 1 or 0. That is the correct output when the market offers fewer clean opportunities.

Scanner settings look right, but R: R fails on everything

The market is likely choppy — support/resistance levels are not clean, making 2:1 R: R difficult to find. This is a signal to reduce trade frequency, not to lower R: R standards.

OPERATOR NOTE

A week with zero qualified setups is a success, not a failure. It means you ran the system correctly, and the market did not offer trades that met your criteria. A week with zero setup costs will cost you nothing. A week where you lower your standards to find trades costs you R. Protecting your capital during low-quality weeks is one of the most profitable things you can do.

The First Sunday Scan: A Walkthrough

The first time running the Sunday scan, give yourself 90 minutes instead of 45. The extra time is for getting familiar with the platform, not because the process is inherently longer. Here is what a first scan looks like from start to finish.

Open Finviz (easiest for a first scan). Apply the filters from the Finviz section above. You get 87 results. Switch to chart view, 20 charts per page. Start with the first page.

Chart 1: AAPL. Strong uptrend, but RSI at 68 — near overbought. No clear consolidation at support. Pass. Chart 2: JPM. Clear horizontal support at $195, tested twice in the past 3 weeks. Volume is declining on the recent pullback. Mark it. Chart 3: A biotech with erratic price action and no discernible structure. Pass immediately.

Continue through 87 charts in approximately 25 minutes. You have flagged 9 candidates. Now the deep review begins.

JPM: You draw the $195 support level. Entry would be $196.50 (above resistance), stop at $193.50 (below support, $0.50 buffer), target at $203 (prior high). R: R = ($203 - $196.50) / ($196.50 - $193.50) = $6.50 / $3.00 = 2.17:1. Passes Criterion 3. Run the full Setup Gate. All five pass. JPM goes on the watchlist.

Of your 9 flagged candidates, 3 pass the full Setup Gate. You have your watchlist for the week. Close the laptop. The scan took 48 minutes. On Monday morning, you will check whether any of the three triggered entry conditions. If they did, you enter once, with the position size calculated from the formula, with GTC orders set immediately. If they did not, check again at 4:30 PM. That is, it is until Tuesday.

OPERATOR NOTE

The Sunday scan is the most important 45 minutes of your trading week. Everything else — Monday entry, daily checks, Friday review — is execution of decisions you made on Sunday in a calm, unhurried state. The quality of your Sunday scan determines the quality of everything that follows. Treat it like the most important meeting of the week, because for your trading account, it is.

GLOSSARY

Average Down

Adding to a losing position to lower the average purchase price. This practice increases the risk of trades already moving against you. The OPERATOR system prohibits this.

Average Volume

The mean daily trading volume over a specified period, typically 20 days. OPERATOR minimum: 1 million shares per day.

Expectancy

The average profit or loss per trade in R units across a large sample. Formula: (Win Rate × Average Win) – (Loss Rate × Average Loss). Positive expectancy means the system profits over time.

GTC Order (Good-Til-Canceled)

An order that remains active until filled or manually canceled. Used to set stops and targets before entry, so the platform executes your plan automatically.

OCO Order (One-Cancels-Other)

A paired order where filling one automatically cancels the other. Used to place stop and target simultaneously — when one triggers, the other cancels.

OPERATOR System

The 8-rule swing trading framework in this book: Setup Gate, size for sleep, define exits, limit checks, never add to losers, take profit at target, survive first loss, review weekly.

PDT Rule (Pattern Day Trader)

SEC regulation requires a minimum $25,000 account balance for accounts that make 4+ round-trip day trades within 5 business days. Does not apply to swing trading.

Position Sizing

The calculation determines how many shares to buy. Formula: (Account Balance × 0.5%) ÷ (Entry Price − Stop Price). Ensures consistent risk per trade regardless of stock price.

R (Risk Unit)

The dollar amount risked by a single trade (entry price minus stop price, multiplied by shares). A +2R result means you gained twice the amount you risked. A -1R result means you lost exactly what you planned.

Resistance

A price level where selling pressure has historically overcome buying pressure, causing the price to stall or reverse. Used as profit targets for long trades.

Risk: Reward Ratio (R: R)

The ratio of potential profit to potential loss. A 2:1 R: R means risking $1 to potentially make $2. OPERATOR minimum: 2:1 on every entry.

Setup Gate

The five-criterion filter every potential trade must pass before entry: Liquidity, Structure, R: R, Market Context, and Conviction.

Spread

The difference between the bid price (what buyers will pay) and the ask price (what sellers want). Wide spreads increase the cost of entering and exiting trades. High-volume stocks have narrower spreads.

Stop Loss

A predefined exit order that closes a position at a specified price when a trade moves against you. Must be placed before entry, at a level where the trade thesis is broken.

Support

A price level where buying pressure has historically overcome selling pressure, causing the price to bounce or reverse. Used as a stop loss placement for long trades.

Swing Trade

A trade held for 2 to 20 trading days, designed to capture a multi-day directional move in a stock while requiring only 2–3 hours per week of active management.

Win Rate

The percentage of trades that reach the profit target. A 55% win rate means 55 of every 100 trades are winners. Positive expectancy is achievable with win rates as low as 40% when R: R is 3:1 or higher.

THE 8 RULES SUMMARY TABLE

All 8 rules work together. Applying 7 of 8 is not the OPERATOR system — it is a customized system that removes the protections the missing rule provides.

THE 8 RULES OF THE OPERATOR SYSTEM

Apply all 8 — every trade, every time. These rules protect each other.

1

RULE #1 — QUALIFY BEFORE ENTRY
Core Principle: The Setup Gate
All 5 criteria must pass before entry.

→ One no = skip. No exceptions, ever.

2

RULE #2 — SIZE FOR SLEEP
Core Principle: Risk 0.5% Per Trade
Never risk more than 0.5% of your account on any single trade.

→ If awake at 3 AM — you are oversized.

3

RULE #3 — DEFINE YOUR EXIT BEFORE ENTRY
Core Principle: Stop and Target First
Set both stop loss and profit target before clicking buy.

→ No exit plan = no trade. Period.

4

RULE #4 — DON'T CHECK CONSTANTLY
Core Principle: Twice Daily Maximum
Pre-market and after close only. Never during market hours.

→ More checking = more chances to override your plan.

5

RULE #5 — NEVER ADD TO LOSERS
Core Principle: Honor the Stop
If wrong at entry, take the planned stop and move on.

→ Averaging down turns small losses into large ones.

6

RULE #6 — TAKE PROFIT AT TARGET
Core Principle: Exit When Price Hits Target
Exit fully when price reaches your predefined target.

→ Greed turns winners into losers. Book the R.

7

RULE #7 — SURVIVE THE FIRST LOSS
Core Principle: Accept — Log — Move On
Accept it, log it honestly, do not revenge trade.

→ How you respond after a loss defines your system.

8

RULE #8 — REVIEW WEEKLY, NOT DAILY
Core Principle: Friday 30-Minute Review
Weekly review every Friday — not daily obsession.

→ Distance creates clarity. Daily reviews create emotion.

PRE-TRADE CHECKLIST — Every Entry

✓ Setup Gate passed   ✓ Size at 0.5% risk   ✓ Stop + target as GTC   ✓ 3 AM test passed   ✓ SPY not in downtrend   ✓ Earnings date checked

These 8 rules are not a menu — they are a system. Apply all 8 or rebuild the expectancy math.   •   OperatorTrading.com

The 8 Rules Summary

Review Weekly, Not Daily

Friday 30-minute review — not a daily obsession

Distance creates clarity. Daily reviews create emotion.

Pre-trade checklist (every entry):

- Setup Gate passed — all 5 criteria confirmed

- Position size calculated at 0.5% risk

- Stop and target placed as GTC orders

- 3 AM test passed — comfortable with the position size

- Market context favorable — SPY not in clear downtrend

- Earnings date checked — no report during planned hold

> **OPERATOR NOTE**
> These 8 rules are not a menu. They are a system. Each rule depends on the others. Position sizing (Rule 2) only works if you have exits predefined (Rule 3). Exit discipline (Rule 3) only holds if you are not constantly checking (Rule 4). The rules protect each other. Apply all 8 or rebuild the expectancy math.

REFERENCES

- Barber, Brad M., and Terrance Odean. 'Trading Is Hazardous to Your Wealth: The Common Stock Investment Performance of Individual Investors.' Journal of Finance 55, no. 2 (2000): 773–806.

- Barber, Brad M., Yi-Tsung Lee, Yu-Jane Liu, and Terrance Odean. 'Do Day Traders Rationally Learn About Their Ability?' Journal of Financial Economics (2017).

- Kahneman, Daniel. Thinking, Fast and Slow. New York: Farrar, Straus and Giroux, 2011.

- Odean, Terrance. 'Do Investors Trade Too Much?' American Economic Review 89, no. 5 (1999): 1279–98.

- Steenbarger, Brett N. The Psychology of Trading: Tools and Techniques for Minding the Markets. Hoboken: Wiley, 2002.

- Steenbarger, Brett N. Enhancing Trader Performance. Hoboken: Wiley, 2006.

- Brokerage data analysis (aggregate anonymized results): 2020–2025. Compiled from publicly available broker disclosures and community trading data.

About the author

Jeff Qualls is an independent trader and educator who specializes in rules-based swing trading systems designed for people with full-time jobs, families, and normal schedules. He teaches that consistent part-time trading is achievable not through complex strategies or constant screen time, but through disciplined rules, conservative position sizing, and patient execution.

Jeff began investing in stocks and ETFs before expanding to options, swing trading, and short-term strategies over a multi-year period. Through consistent application of rules-based methods, he developed the OPERATOR system — a practical framework for traders who want results without sacrificing the rest of their lives.

As a career educator (college and high school CTE programs, ages 14+), Jeff emphasizes practical financial literacy, discipline, and realistic expectations. He has coached traders from retail workers starting with $500 to engineers with six-figure accounts, consistently finding that the rules-based approach works across all account sizes and life circumstances.

Through the OPERATOR series, Jeff demystifies trading, empowers individuals to control their financial futures, and inspires a mindset shift from hoping the market works for you to building systems that do.

DON'T FORGET YOUR FREE WORKBOOK

You've learned the 8 Rules system. Now get the FREE 43-page workbook that helps you execute it:

- ☐ Setup Gate checklist

- ☐ Position sizing calculator

- ☐ Trade logs

- ☐ Weekly review templates

- ☐ Risk management worksheets

Download free at: OperatorTrading.com/workbook.

THE OPERATOR SERIES AND NEXT STEPS

This is Volume 1 in the OPERATOR series. For deeper dives:

- OPERATOR Volume 2 (Zero to Trader): Advanced execution, market structure, sector rotation, earnings plays, performance psychology. Assumes you know the 8 rules — goes deeper into execution under pressure.

- Workbook (OperatorTrading.com/workbook): Printable templates, trackers, dashboards, and the Setup Gate checklist in wallet-card format.

- OPERATOR Coaching ($97/month): Weekly group sessions, trade reviews, personalized feedback, pattern recognition, and accountability.

Trade without panic. Live with freedom.

Jeff Qualls

April 2026

Intentionally Blank